Ethnic Heritage in Mississippi

Fondly,
Barbara Carpenter

Columbus lands in the "New World" and encounters the Native Americans as
King Ferdinand watches and points. Woodcut from the "Columbus Letter"
(Guiliano Dati's *La Lettera Dellisole*, 1493). Library of Congress.

Ethnic Heritage in

MISSISSIPPI

EDITED BY

BARBARA CARPENTER

PUBLISHED FOR
THE MISSISSIPPI HUMANITIES COUNCIL
BY
THE UNIVERSITY PRESS OF MISSISSIPPI
JACKSON AND LONDON

95 94 93 92   4 3 2 1

The paper in this book meets the guidelines for permanence and durability of the
Committee on Production Guidelines for Book Longevity of the Council on Library
Resources.

Library of Congress Cataloging-in-Publication Data

Ethnic heritage in Mississippi / edited by Barbara Carpenter.
    p. cm.
    Includes bibliographical references and index.
    ISBN 0-87805-578-9 (alk. paper)
    1. Minorities—Mississippi—History. 2. Mississippi—Race
relations. 3. Mississippi—Ethnic relations. I. Carpenter,
Barbara. II. Mississippi Humanities Council.
F350.A1E84 1992
976.2'004—dc20   92-5655
                                                        CIP

British Library Cataloging-in-Publication data available

Contents

Preface

Commemoration seems to be a necessary part of human nature, both in individuals and in societies, to mark occasions of significance and preserve memory and history. Long before any written records were kept, festivities were held at such times as the harvest, mid-winter, and the solstices, and even though most of us in 1992 have become less attuned to these natural seasons we still tend to celebrate birthdays, anniversaries, and communal events.

Ideas of celebration change, however. The U.S. Centennial in 1876, only a decade after the ravages of civil war, centered almost entirely and perhaps a little defensively on Philadelphia and the special history surrounding the Declaration of Independence, with slight attention to other elements of the American experience. A hundred years later, in 1976, the country attempted a more pluralistic, locally-conceived celebration and, indeed, achieved it, with everything from fireworks displays, parades, and regattas of tall ships to patriotically painted fire hydrants in every small town. The 1893 Columbian Exposition, though it became extremely significant in influencing American architecture, museums, entertainment, and the culture in general, apparently had little to do with Christopher Columbus or even with history, at least in the minds of the general public, and has been most widely known as the Chicago World's Fair.

As the five hundredth anniversary of Columbus's first voyage approaches, some thoughtful citizens have suggested that a more serious component of its commemoration would be appropriate, one which would seek to provide a perspective on the landfall of October 12, 1492, and on the then unimaginable and even now incalculable consequences of that event. Not denying, at least at first, the place of tee shirts, picnics, and decorated balloons, they argued that the significance of such occasions far too often gets lost in the hullabaloo, and that plans should include scholarly research into the past which leads, among other things, to educational programs and exhibits to bring to the typical American citizen some notion of the occasion's importance to the entire course of human history—along with the festivities.

It soon became clear, however, that this was not to be a simple process. While few would object to commemoration of some kind, many began to come forward to protest that the Quincentenary was not necessarily an occasion for celebration. Celebration, they insisted, implies events worth extolling, and ignores the less savory aspects of the history in question. Thus as public planners, scholars, and civic-minded individuals came together, not always harmoniously, to make plans, assessment and taking of stock suddenly came about very naturally. These leaders confronted the multifaceted nature of society and of history in this country, intentionally or not. This increased awareness of the scope of our country's ethnic heritage may ultimately prove to be the most enduring legacy of the Quincentenary.

Time magazine in the October 7, 1991, issue summed up the controversies in its usual facile and succinct fashion: "1. Columbus' journey was the first step in a process that produced a daring experiment in democracy, which in turn became a symbol and a haven of liberty. Or . . . 2. Indigenous peoples were doomed by European arrogance, brutality, and infectious diseases. Columbus' gift was slavery to those who greeted him; his arrival set in motion the ruthless destruction of the natural world he entered."

Time's statement is simplistic. Yet it states in very concise form the sometimes violently conflicting attitudes of the many groups who have come forward to express opinions and agendas. The Roman Catholic Church views the occasion as an opportunity to celebrate the evangelization of the people of the Americas and the tremendous expansion of Christianity. But other groups, perhaps most notably the National Council of Churches of Christ, insist that the event marks a sordid episode of racism and exploitism for Christians. Hispanics make an impassioned plea that this anniversary provides a chance to redress some of the degradation they have endured because of the "black legend." But perhaps the most insistent protests have come from Native Americans. The Congress of American Indians has called 1492 the beginning of the "Western Hemisphere holocaust" and is celebrating 1491 as the last year before the European invasion. Native Americans all across the country have decreed October 12 a day of mourning.

But what does this have to do with Mississippi? The Mississippi Humanities Council could not be unaware of these conflicting attitudes as it planned programs around the Quincentenary. Issues that surfaced nationally are evident in this state, whose past demonstrates in microcosm the conflicts and adjustments between Native Americans and Europeans and those precipitated by the only slightly later arrival of Africans and the quite recent influx of a significant number of Asians. Though Mississippi is often considered a black-and-white state, even by its own residents, its population includes a significant number of ethnic groups who have made fundamental and pervasive contributions to the development of the Mississippi culture of the late twentieth century. As the Council considered what its thrust should be in funding programs related to the Quincentenary, it became increasingly clear that projects studying ethnic diversity must be a major component of programming. Additionally, this diversity must be demonstrated as integral to the entire history of the state, from the indigenous people who were here when the Europeans first arrived to the latest newcomers. Finally, the effects of their interactions, their "encounters" to use the Quincentenary's considered term, should be investigated from many perspectives. Thus this project.

The book has two goals. First of all, it is intended to present current scholarship and contemporary approaches to portions of the state's history that have traditionally been given scant attention in most textbooks and scholarly writing about Mississippi. It is also intended to serve as a starting point for public programs of many different kinds that are appropriate for Humanities Council sponsorship. The essays themselves were solicited from outstanding scholars in their fields to provide the latest research. They outline in brief the history of groups that comprise today's Mississippians. They are written to highest academic standards but in a style accessible to the interested general reader. This was the challenge faced by our contributors, one they have met head-on with remarkable success.

The first section deals with the original Native Americans, setting the stage with an overview of prehistoric Mississippi, moving through analysis of protohistoric and early historic periods, and finally focusing on the history of the Choctaws, the only Indian tribe still present in significant numbers in Mississippi today. The second section moves to the coming of Europeans. The first essay in that group considers what Europe was like and what was taking place there as Columbus set out. Subsequent essays discuss early exploration and colonization, concluding with a discussion of the Africans who came—or were brought—to Mississippi, mostly as slaves. A final documentary photographic essay surveys ethnic groups in contemporary Mississippi, providing a brief history of each group and analyzing their techniques for balancing their cultural heritage and their commitment to what is for many their native state and country.

Most of the typical points of dissension that have surfaced in the last few years nationally and internationally are explicit in these essays; others are implicit but nonetheless clear. We have attempted to be sensitive to the concerns of all portions of our society, knowing omniscience to be impossible. We can willingly concede that the significance of the voyage is not what Columbus "found" but what happened as a consequence. We see the validity of the views of those who protest that the voluntary coming of Europeans and forced advent of Africans engendered disease, loss of homeland, depopulation, disappearance of traditional ways. We also see ourselves as the beneficiaries of those sturdy Europeans who came and settled and established the basis for the state as we know it, in language, forms of government, and the ways many of us perceive ourselves.

Of necessity, a plethora of fascinating possibilities remain unexplored. Some may not appear to relate directly to Mississippi—the real character and motivation of Columbus, for instance, or the "truth" of the black legend, or even the effects of the supposed "new" world on the old. Yet others impinge directly on our lives five hundred years later—changes in the world's ecology, instantaneous communication in the global village, Mississippi's links with Latin America, our sister land which often seems alien in language and many other ways. We hope that as we read and discuss the essays other questions will arise which should be important to us—attitudes toward other, different cultures, tolerance toward groups in our own society which we do not know well.

But most of all, we hope that these essays will begin to demonstrate the multiplicity of people, circumstances, and events which have contributed to what is now Mississippi. Though we may all mourn some elements of our past, private and collective, we can surely celebrate the deep roots, strong branches, and beautiful many-colored leaves that comprise the Mississippi family tree in 1992.

Barbara Carpenter
December 1991

Acknowledgments

So many people have contributed to this project, from inception and planning through final publication, that I can mention only a few of the most notable. I first want to thank the National Endowment for the Humanities, which funded the book through an Exemplary Award to the Mississippi Humanities Council. In particular I thank Carole Watson, Director of the Division of State Programs, and Tim Matthewson, Program Officer, for their advice and encouragement over the long haul. We could not have done this without you.

Charles Lowery has been an invaluable source of information and encouragement in all phases of this project, from developing the proposal to editing the final text. Patricia Galloway contributed expertise and creative advice from start to finish. John Peterson did the same, and could not escape our questions even in Zimbabwe. All the contributors have been extremely prompt and cooperative and a pleasure to work with. The Editorial Board gave thorough attention and thoughtful suggestions; I am particularly appreciative of Ken Carleton's help with Choctaw names and spelling. Ray Skates's insightful and detailed comments kept us on course at several junctures.

Sources for graphics are acknowledged with the illustrations, and numerous people and organizations assisted us in locating often obscure pictures, maps, and other materials. A special thanks goes to the staff of the Mississippi Department of Archives and History, many of whom went far out of their way to be helpful: Elaine Owens, Ken P'Pool, Cavett Taff, Jo Miles-Seely, Mary Lohrenz, and Anne Lipscomb in particular deserve mention. Frances Boeckman and John Magill made special efforts on our behalf, as did Susan Danforth, Mark Thiel, Beth Koostra, Jeffrey Robbins, Tom Rankin, Jay Mitchell, Sam Brookes, Ray Claycomb, Jim Dawson, and the staffs at the Information Services Library and Eudora Welty Library in Jackson. Robert E. Hauberg, Jr., reviewed the contract and gave permission to reproduce a print in his collection. Charles Weeks gave unstintingly of his time and research, as well as advice on spelling of Spanish names; many of his ideas are fundamental to this project.

The idea would not have been birthed nor the proposal written without the support of the Mississippi Humanities Council members and staff. The Council's consistent interest in serving and preserving the heritage of all Mississippians is at the root of the project, and their insistence on excellence in programming gives it shape. Cora Norman, Brenda Gray, and Celia Booth made prodigious efforts during the three year gestation period. Barbara Carroon, Project Coordinator, devoted her considerable energies, attention to detail, sagacious observations, and cheerful willingness to undertake absolutely anything to do this book, and it would not have been completed without her assistance. And T. W. Lewis, III, like Maria Gostrey, "saw me through." I cannot thank you all enough.

PART ONE

SETTING THE STAGE
The Original Mississippians

Introduction

John H. Peterson, Jr.

The opening chapters of this book focus on the original inhabitants of Mississippi, the American Indians, and specifically on the only surviving Indian group, the Mississippi Choctaws. The diversity in these first four chapters demonstrates the unique position of American Indians in the ethnic diversity of Mississippi. Too often Indian Americans are mentioned at the beginning of state histories before being relegated to the dust bin of history.

The Indians' place in Mississippi ethnicity is suggested by much more than their numbers within the population of the state. The Indians are the only group whose long prehistoric development occurred within our state boundaries. Probably few of us wonder much about the prehistoric development of the immigrant ethnic groups from Europe and Africa and other parts of the world. A picture of Stonehenge or some other spectacular ruin is perhaps all most of us know of the prehistory behind the modern cultures which sent our ancestors as immigrants to Mississippi. All of these groups underwent their own paths of development and change, of increased utilization of the environment, and of growth of larger settlements and centralized governments. We ignore the prehistory of most ethnic groups since their distant past took place on other continents. Somehow, overseas prehistory does not seem part of our American or Mississippian heritage whether our ancestors came from Europe or Africa. But the Indians are different. Their prehistoric remains still dot the landscape of Mississippi. Their ancient tools still are occasionally found in the fields or even in backyard gardens in new suburbs. Indian prehistory is part of the landscape in Mississippi, much as Indian place names are part of Mississippi geography.

It is easy to dismiss this as the ancient past of a now small ethnic group. But most of us have some natural curiosity about what lies behind the construction of the mounds found in much of Mississippi, or who used these artifacts found in our museums if not now in our own yards and fields. What is the meaning of the Indian past, not just for Indian Mississippians but for all of us?

Archaeologist Jay Johnson attempts in the first essay to help us see with the eye of a cultural historian an entire vanished way of life. Basing his discussion on physical remains in the ground and artifacts left behind, Johnson describes not just the Indians first met by the newly arriving Europeans, but an Indian past stretching back thousands of years. He describes a period when the Indians themselves were few in number and the land was still inhabited by animals such as the mammoths that are unknown to living peoples. He describes the early Indians as a nomadic people still moving from one resource to another depending on annual and seasonal availability of these resources. Johnson shares with us the tantalizing physical evidence which is all that is available to answer questions about where these people came from, how they lived, and what they believed.

Johnson describes how the remains of these early Indians show a gradual development of a more settled way of life, of increased population, of increased use of materials representing trade with other areas. He demonstrates how these developments in the later Woodland period formed the basis for a complex culture based on agricultural production of corn, beans, and squash. Populations increased and villages became larger. In the larger population centers, there was a centralization of political and religious authority and an extension of control over outlying regions.

The Indians of Mississippi followed the same long development over thousands of years that other peoples elsewhere in the world followed, from scattered hunters to agriculturalists to members of complex and dynamic cultures. Some scholars might not consider the more complex North American Indian societies civilized since they did not possess writing, which the dictionary lists as one criterion of civilization. But the Mississippian Indian societies certainly met other criteria of civilization, such as advanced agricultural technology, expanded populations, and a complex social organization.

It is not important to compare the prehistorical development of Mississippi Indians with that of other groups. The more important point is that in Mississippi we have evidence of the same course of development toward complex civil societies among Indian Americans as that which took place in other continents for the ancestors of other ethnic groups currently inhabiting our state. This archaeological record is not just the unique record of Indian prehistory. It is to some extent the record of all peoples whose ancestors followed similar courses towards historical times.

Most of us will never visit the great prehistorical sites on other continents and try to envision the slow generation-by-generation changes of peoples and cultures as they emerged into written history. But we can stand at archaeological sites in Mississippi such as the Winterville Mounds, Nanih Waiya, and the Emerald Mound. We can visit similar sites in adjacent states such as Poverty Point, Louisiana, and Moundville, Alabama. At these places we can try to understand the effort by generation after generation of Mississippi Indians to develop a way of life for themselves and their descendants, and perhaps thereby we can also gain some understanding of the gradual development of other human societies, including the European and African societies whose prehistoric remains are distant from our shores. Johnson's article closes with the hope that an appreciation for Mississippi archaeological sites will lead to a recognition that the archaeological record is fragile. It can be destroyed before the results are preserved and interpreted. It is not just the prehistory of Mississippi Indians which lies in the archaeological record, it is the history of human-kind.

In the second paper, Patricia Galloway examines the difficult question of the relationship between the peoples who left the remains studied by archaeologists and the historical Indian tribes described by early explorers. Unfortunately, there is often no simple and direct link between archaeologically known cultures and historically described societies. This transition from the archaeological past to the historical past is rendered more difficult because of the massive impact of the early Spanish explorers. In 1991, as many Americans prepare for the five-hundredth anniversary of the first voyage of Christopher Columbus, major controversies have been featured in news magazines and popular periodicals. The significance of the "Columbus event" on world history hardly needs celebrating. The ocean voyages between the "old" world and the "new" world were responsible for bringing to this continent the ancestors of all non-Indian ancestors of the current population of Mississippians. Whether our ancestors came from Europe, Africa, or Asia, free or slave, most of them still came from somewhere else. Their arrival on this continent marked a decisive change in their lives as well as the lives of us, their descendants. But the arrival of the explorers and then settlers made an equally decisive impact on the complex societies of the Mississippi Indians. For these native Americans, contact with Spanish explorers and European diseases was a disaster which largely destroyed their population centers prior to contact by later settlers who wrote much of the early history of the region.

The downfall of the classical Mississippian Indian societies was largely un-observed and until recently not understood. Galloway has combined recent research in southeastern archaeology and comparative studies of societies from anthropology with her extensive knowledge of the earliest historical documents to describe the Indian people of the southeast before and after the destruction and their efforts at reorganization following contact. She provides a full description of the classical Mississippian society and then explains the tragedy which accompanied contact with Europeans. In the disintegration of the larger population centers, there followed a complex pattern of population movement and amalgamation from which emerged the historically known and named Indian tribes of Mississippi.

Galloway describes the southeastern Indians as fortunate in not possessing obvious wealth in gold or other resources which attracted the massive European colonial effort in Hispaniola, Mexico, and Peru. As a result, during the seventeenth and eighteenth centuries the Indians of the southeast were able to adapt to their changed circumstances and begin exercising some degree of control over the economic and military competition between European powers. This degree of Indian control and adaptation did not begin to erode until the balance of population and military power shifted to the emerging dominant power in the southeast, the "American" nation.

Historian Sam Wells presents the story of the transition of the Choctaws from an autonomous nation to an ethnic group within the boundaries of the United States. His focus is on the treaties signed between the Choctaws and the United States from the Treaty of Hopewell in 1786 to the Treaty of Dancing Rabbit Creek in 1830, which required Choctaw removal from Mississippi. As Wells points out, from the beginning, the Choctaws were defined as occupying land within what the U.S. considered American territory. The subsequent treaties show a pattern of gradual increase in the authority of the United States over the Choctaws as well as a continuous secession of lands by the Choctaws.

The Choctaws made major efforts to accommodate themselves to becoming part of the larger American nation by requesting in these treaties such resources as mission schools and instruction in agricultural technology. In spite of these efforts and the Choctaws' loyal support of the Americans in the Creek War as part of the War of 1812, white citizens of the new state of Mississippi did not want another sovereign nation within Mississippi. In the Treaty of Doaks' Stand in 1820, the U.S. "compensated" the Choctaws with land west of the Mississippi in return for land in Mississippi and Alabama. Experiencing continued pressure from the Mississippi legislature, the Choctaws appealed to the U.S. Congress. But the national government had embarked on a policy of Indian removal from the southeast with the passage of the Indian Removal Act of 1830, which led directly to the Treaty of Dancing Rabbit Creek in September 1830. Many Choctaws preferred to remain in Mississippi, but their efforts to register for land were rejected by the federal Indian agent, William Ward.

The Choctaws were the first Indian tribe to be removed from the southeast. Choctaw removal has not generally received the historical attention devoted to the later removal of the Cherokees. This omission was possible partially because the Choctaw removal took place in several stages, but it was no less tearful and difficult than later Indian removals. The Choctaws who remained in Mississippi were subject to continuous harassment, such as burning of their homes and stealing of their cattle. Gradually all but the most traditional and determined Choctaws gave up and left for Oklahoma. Wells closes by noting that a recurring theme in U.S.-Choctaw relationships is the betrayal of trust and sacrifice of one people's liberty for the benefit of another. A reasonable question is the degree to which this may be a basic theme in U.S. history for other ethnic groups as well.

In the final paper dealing with the Indian people of Mississippi, historian and Oklahoma Choctaw Clara Sue Kidwell provides a detailed description of the Choctaws as a community of people. Her description of the Choctaws begins in the early part of the nineteenth century, when the reorganization described by Galloway was largely complete and adaptation to American society was well underway. The efforts of the Choctaw people to accommodate to the increasing power of the United States and white Americans' greed for

Choctaw land are described, as is the impact on the Choctaw people of the
national policy of Indian removal.

In Kidwell's paper, the Choctaw people cease to be prehistoric cultures and
archaeological sites, or emerging historical people, or even a political entity.
Kidwell describes people, who they are, where they lived, who their leaders
were, and how they tried to respond to the major changes that affected them.
She takes her story beyond the disruption of removal following the Treaty of
Dancing Rabbit Creek in 1830 to a second disruption of the Choctaws at the
end of the nineteenth century as part of the dissolution of the Choctaw Nation
in Oklahoma. But in spite of this later tragedy for the remaining Choctaws,
Kidwell demonstrates that the remaining Mississippi Choctaws were beginning to emerge and develop their own place in Mississippi society. They continued to live in their own communities, maintaining their own language and
customs, but were becoming more a part of the culture and society of the state
as a whole. It was on the basis of these rural farming communities that the
Choctaws began to reemerge in the twentieth century, first through the development of the Choctaw Reservation and Choctaw tribal government, and in
recent decades into the economic development programs which have made the
Mississippi Choctaws a model for Indian development throughout the nation.

Prehistoric Mississippi

Jay K. Johnson

Early in the winter of 1973, Sam Brookes, an archaeologist who has been working in Mississippi since the late 1960s, first visited the Hester Site, an ancient campsite on the banks of the Tombigbee near Aberdeen in northeastern Mississippi. Brookes had seen collections of artifacts from the site which contained several Dalton points, a distinctive stone spear point that has been dated to 8500 B.C. The site had been vandalized; gaping holes and crooked trenches marked the fact that important information about some of the oldest inhabitants of Mississippi was being destroyed. Artifacts were being removed into private collections without study, and all of the data that could have been derived from a detailed study of the arrangement of the artifacts in the ground was being lost.

At that time Brookes was working for the Mississippi Department of Archives and History, which recognized the importance of the Hester Site and authorized three months of excavation. A portion of the site that had not been destroyed was carefully exposed and recorded. Hundreds of tools and the debris of everyday life were found and studied. Data from Hester confirmed information gathered elsewhere in the Southeastern United States on the way

9

Hester Site, early archaic point chronology.
Courtesy of Samuel O. Brookes.

of life for these early inhabitants of Mississippi. The people who made and used Dalton spear points were the last of what archaeologists call Paleo-Indians. Earlier in the period, PaleoIndians concentrated on hunting big game, including bison and mammoth. Although big game kill sites have not been discovered in Mississippi, spear points that are similar to the ones used to kill bison in other states have been found.

By Dalton times, big game appears to have died out in Mississippi, some say through overhunting. At any rate, evidence from Hester indicates that the earliest inhabitants there had shifted the focus of their hunting to deer, an emphasis that would characterize the rest of prehistory in Mississippi. The Dalton hunters used tools and techniques that they learned from their big game hunting ancestors. Dalton and other PaleoIndian spear point types are found sporadically throughout Mississippi in situations that suggest that this group was using the landscape in a different way than would the people who came after them.

The PaleoIndian period was followed by the Archaic, a relatively stable pattern of adaptation that lasted for nearly 7000 years. Brookes was able to relate the Dalton points to other tools used by the earliest inhabitants at Hester through their association in the same deposits. In the upper levels of the site, he was able to document several younger, Early Archaic occupations. Relatively few stratified sites have been excavated in Mississippi, and Hester provided the opportunity to study the transition from PaleoIndian to Archaic in one spot.

The Archaic tool kit appears to have been much more generalized. Spear points were still important, but other tools used in processing large animals had been replaced by tools used to prepare other foods. A common Archaic tool was a two- to three-pound stone with shallow depressions where large numbers of hickory nuts were cracked. Charred nutshells, other plant remains, and bones found in Archaic sites document dependence on a broader range of plants and animals during this period.

Still, the remains of permanent structures are uncommon in Archaic sites, indicating that Indians in Mississippi continued to be nomadic, moving from one resource zone to another, responding to seasonal availability. This general pattern held throughout the Archaic, with a gradual change in spear point style which allows archaeologists to tell Early, Middle, and Late Archaic sites apart. There was also a gradual increase in population. Late Archaic points are much more common than Early Archaic points throughout the state.

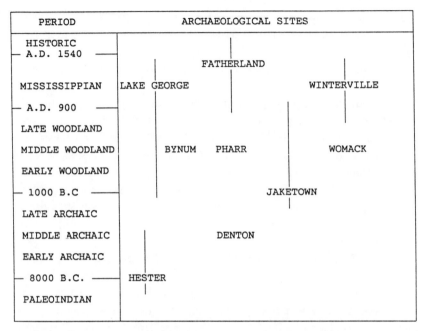

PERIOD	ARCHAEOLOGICAL SITES
HISTORIC A.D. 1540 —	FATHERLAND
MISSISSIPPIAN	LAKE GEORGE WINTERVILLE
— A.D. 900 —	
LATE WOODLAND	
MIDDLE WOODLAND	BYNUM PHARR WOMACK
EARLY WOODLAND	
— 1000 B.C —	JAKETOWN
LATE ARCHAIC	
MIDDLE ARCHAIC	DENTON
EARLY ARCHAIC	
— 8000 B.C. —	HESTER
PALEOINDIAN	

Prehistoric chronology in Mississippi and selected archaeological sites. Courtesy of Jay K. Johnson.

There are indicators of an increase in social complexity during some parts of the Archaic. For example, late in the Middle Archaic, at about 3600 B.C., a distinctive stone found in the middle Tennessee River Valley and used in spear point manufacture was traded throughout the north half of Mississippi. At the same time groups of unusually large and well-made spear points were buried in what may have been human burial contexts in the upper Tombigbee drainage. These artifacts were clearly ceremonial items because their size, often three times as long as the standard spear point, and their thinness make it impossible for them to have been used for hunting and cutting tasks. It is uncertain if they were grave offerings, because only a few have been recovered by archaeologists. At the same time, in northwestern Mississippi at the Denton Site near Clarksdale, Archaic peoples were making elaborate stone beads by grinding extremely hard local material.

The complex ritual implied by the non-utilitarian Middle Archaic artifacts was followed by a significant development at the very end of the Archaic period. At the Poverty Point site across the river from Vicksburg near Epps, Louisiana, at about 1000 B.C., Indians literally carved the landscape, cutting and filling to create a series of concentric ridges surrounding a plaza nearly 2000 feet wide. In addition to the ridges, earth mounds containing thousands of cubic yards of dirt were constructed. Exotic goods such as copper, galena, soapstone, quartz crystals, and other stones were gathered from throughout the eastern United States, brought to Poverty Point, and transformed into artifacts that could only have been useful for rituals. Poverty Point artifacts and mounds are found elsewhere in Mississippi, primarily in the Delta but also on the Gulf coast. The Mississippi remains are not as elaborate as those across the river. Still, sites like Jaketown and Slate near Belzoni and Claiborne and Cedarland Plantation near Bay Saint Louis have yielded an elaborate set of nonutilitarian artifacts made from exotic raw materials.

Archaeologists have made a major effort to understand Poverty Point remains in Louisiana and Mississippi. These sites present a problem because too much happened too soon. Ceremonial architecture, long distance trade, and ritual paraphernalia of this scale and complexity do not occur again in the Southeast for another 2000 years. At this later time, they are accompanied by clear evidence for intensive agriculture. During the 1950s it was thought that agriculture must have been the basis for subsistence at Poverty Point. However, as more food samples from Poverty Point trash deposits were analyzed, it became clear that this was not the case. In the thousands of pieces of charred plants that have been examined, not one piece of corn or bean has been found. It is obvious that the Poverty Point peoples made full use of the unusually rich environment of the lower Mississippi River Valley. Why the people who followed in the same region were not as successful in organizing large groups of laborers to build public monuments is not clear.

At Jaketown and other Poverty Point Period sites, archaeologists have found a few pieces of pots made by mixing plant fibers into the clay before it was shaped or fired. This is some of the earliest pottery found in the Southeast. It was replaced rather quickly by ceramics made from clay mixed with sand or other material. The introduction of ceramics marks the beginning of the Woodland Period. Archaeologists have concentrated on the pieces of broken pottery which characterize Woodland and later sites because they are an excellent source of information about exactly when a particular site was occupied. The decoration on pots changed through time in a regular way, so that most of the ceramics from a given period are similar to each other but are different from those which came before or after.

Ceramics are also often considered an indicator of a more fundamental change in the way of life. According to this argument, clay vessels are heavy and fragile and thus would be unlikely tools for a group of people who move their place of residence regularly. Therefore, pottery signifies the beginning of permanent settlement. However, analysis of the food remains and tools from Early Woodland sites shows little to distinguish them from Late Archaic sites. Except for the presence of pot fragments, they are about the same, part of a continuum from relatively less to relatively more reliance on plant food. In fact, it was during the Woodland Period that the reliance on locally available plants became rather intense. Large sites from the end of the period give every indication of permanent settlement and the exploitation of a full range of plants. Some native plants, sunflower and various grasses for example, had been domesticated. Deer continued to be a major source of protein.

Archaeologists have also found a good sample of the remains of domestic structures at Woodland sites. These houses usually had a circular floor plan outlined by a series of round stains left in the soil when the posts rotted. There was often a central hearth, and sometimes remains of an entrance way is marked by two short, parallel lines of post stains perpendicular to the outer wall. These were not temporary structures built by people who planned to stay at a site for only a few weeks.

Earthen mound construction continued during the Woodland but, until late in the period, most of the mounds were relatively small, conical constructions that were built to include the remains of the dead. Sometimes, as at the Bynum Mounds near Houston in northeast Mississippi, the mounds were the result of a single construction episode, made to cover a central tomb which was dug into the old land surface and covered with logs. Sometimes the mounds re-sulted from several building episodes, with each addition including another burial or group of burials. The Womack Mound near Coffeeville in north central Mississippi is a good example of this practice. Sometimes, there is a combination of the two, with a central tomb and individual burials spread throughout the mound, as was evident at the Pharr Mounds near Tishomingo in northeast Mississippi.

Since there were not enough mounds to hold the growing population of the Woodland, and there were burials within the villages themselves, there is the implication that the mounds were constructed as special burial places for

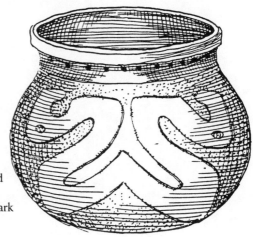

Example of Middle Woodland bird effigy pot from Bynum Mound. Courtesy National Park Service.

the important people in each settlement. The ceramic vessels that often accompany the burials support this assumption, since nothing like them is found in the village trash deposits. These vessels often show elaborate, abstract depictions of birds that are nearly identical to designs found on pots from similar contexts at sites in the Ohio River Valley. There was obviously some sort of communication of religious ideas that occurred throughout the eastern United States, particularly during the Early and Middle Woodland. Other kinds of communication are evident in the burial of artifacts made from Gulf coast conch shell and Great Lakes copper in the mounds. Beads and pendants were made from conch shell while ear ornaments and pan pipes were made from copper. Although these and other exotic materials are fairly common in the mounds, they are rarely found in the villages. Long distance trade was only important in securing valuable goods in order to mark high status individuals in death and, presumably, in life.

The distinction between commoner and elite becomes much more important during the succeeding Mississippi Period. This period begins at about A.D. 900 and is named after the Mississippi River, since the river valley from St. Louis south was heavily populated during this time. This settlement location is a direct reflection of a major change in subsistence. One of the things that distinguishes the Mississippi Period is a reliance on corn, beans, and squash agriculture. These crops were derived from Central America and are

"Downtown Clarksdale Circa 1540." The painting can be viewed at the Carnegie Public Library in Clarksdale. Courtesy Carnegie Public Library. Photograph courtesy of Tom Rankin.

easiest to grow in the rich soils of the flood plains. Large river valleys throughout the Southeast contain abundant Mississippian sites, and they are common in the Delta and major river valleys such as the Black, Pearl, and Tombigbee. They are rare in upland oak-pine forests of north and central Mississippi and the piney woods of south Mississippi.

The introduction of agriculture transformed the landscape in many ways. In the first place, larger numbers of people could live in those areas where agriculture was possible using prehistoric techniques. Mississippian sites are frequently huge, covering several acres. Upon excavation, they reveal rectangular house patterns that are often located around a plaza or central cleared area, as they were at the Wilsford Site near Clarksdale in the Delta. Often a large portion of the village was enclosed within a wall made by setting large vertical posts close together in the ground. The Lake George Site near Belzoni had a moat as well as a wall, a portion of which has been excavated. These palisades clearly had a defensive function. Other evidence for Mississippian Period warfare includes burials with stone arrow points in the rib cage or embedded in the bones of the skull or hip, uninhabited buffer zones between groups of sites serving as an apparent no man's land, and warrior representations in Mississippian art.

Aerial view of Emerald Mound, located just off the Natchez Trace above Natchez. Built by reshaping a hill, Emerald is one of the largest mounds in the Southeast. Photograph by Don Black. Courtesy of National Park Service.

The strongest evidence of the increase in population and the centralization of control in larger Mississippian villages was the construction of large earthen mounds. The Mississippians continued to build conical burial mounds and placed in them burials containing grave goods that were no less elaborate but in a different style from those of the Woodland mounds. However, the characteristic Mississippian mound form was the truncated pyramid or platform mound. Excavation of these mounds usually reveals a special structure at the summit which must have served as a chief's house or temple. The temple mound characteristically faced onto the plaza that was at the heart of the village, and the implications of this location for public ceremony are clear.

Since most of the Mississippian sites are located in relatively flat alluvial valleys, the entire mounds were man made. Many of these temple mounds are quite large. The principal mound at the Winterville Site, just north of Greenville, is more than fifty-five feet high. Sometimes features of the local topography could be incorporated. The Emerald Mound, on the Natchez Trace to the north of Natchez, became one of the largest Mississippian mounds in the Southeast by incorporating and reshaping a hill.

The focus of the villages around the temple mounds nicely symbolizes the centralization of authority that is characteristic of Mississippian society. Archaeological data in combination with the accounts of early European explorers make it clear that Mississippian society was non-egalitarian. There was a priestly class whose membership was determined by birth. These people served as both religious and political leaders and were buried in the mounds. Rather than occasional individuals who rose to high status as reflected in their burial in mounds, there was now an entire segment of society whose membership was, in some cases, a birthright.

The chroniclers of Hernando de Soto's trek across the Southeast in the middle of the sixteenth century documented many aspects of Mississippian social organization. At Quizquiz, one of the principle villages encountered in the Delta, the chief with whom Soto dealt lived atop a flat topped mound.

Additional information on the internal workings of Mississippian society comes from the French colonial documents on the Natchez. The Fatherland site in present day Natchez is a fairly typical Mississippian mound site that was occupied by the Great Sun, chief of the Natchez, during the early part of the French occupation in the eighteenth century. The Natchez were an unusually resilient example of Mississippian society. Most chiefdoms collapsed quite early in the historic period under the pressures of disease and warfare which came with European contact. The Delta was densely populated when Soto crossed it in 1541 but nearly deserted by the time of the La Salle expedition in 1682.

In this abbreviated account, it is difficult to avoid giving the impression of steady and almost inevitable evolution of culture. From the Archaic through the Woodland to the Mississippian there is clear evidence for a gradually more sophisticated use of the environment, allowing larger and larger population aggregates. Increasingly more centralized government is needed as more and more people live together in one spot year round. This in turn seems to have led to increased complexity in other aspects of culture such as long distance trade, craft specialization, ceremonialism, and architecture.

However, when the archaeological record is examined more closely, local episodes of advance in cultural complexity become evident. Each of these is punctuated by intervals in which there is relatively little evidence of centralization of political control or elaborate ritual. In fact, there is good evidence that the Mississippian chiefdoms encountered by the first explorers were in the process of change. Sometime during the fifteenth century, before first contact, the Chickasaw in northeastern Mississippi had shifted their settlement from large village locations in the river bottoms to small hamlets in the uplands of the Black Prairie. At about the same time, they quit building temple mounds.

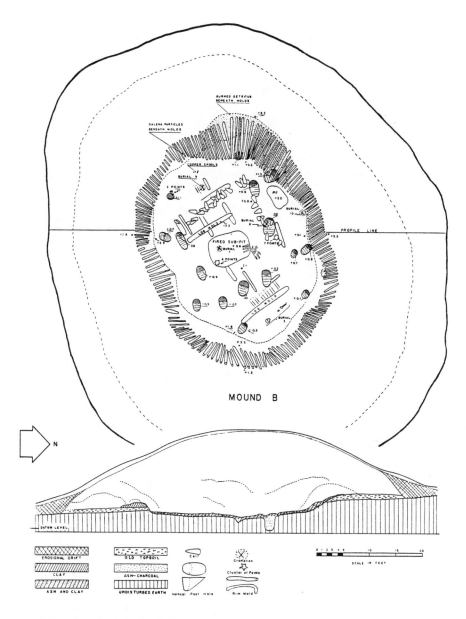

MOUND B

This archaeologist's sketch indicates the enormous detail available to a trained eye. Courtesy of National Park Service.

This decentralization of settlement implies a decentralization of authority, a transformation which cannot be attributed to European disruption and which, in fact, may have had a role in making the Chickasaw a major political force in colonial Mississippi.

The archaeological record makes it clear that the Indian cultures encountered by European explorers and settlers in Mississippi were the result of thousands of years of change and adaptation to the local environment. Some of this adaptation was immediately evident to the settlers, who borrowed freely from the Indians in adjusting European culture to the new land. Archaeologists are just beginning to understand other aspects of the complex and dynamic native cultures of Mississippi. Much more can be learned about the prehistory of the state as archaeological research methods improve. But research into prehistory depends on a limited and fragile resource, the archaeological record itself. There will never be any more Hester Sites.

SUGGESTED READINGS

Cotter, John L., and John M. Corbett. *Archeology of the Bynum Mounds Mississippi.* Archeological Research Series, National Park Service, U.S. Department of the Interior, Washington. 1951.

Gibson, Jon L. "The Poverty Point Earthworks Reconsidered," *Mississippi Archeology* (1987) 22(2):14–32.

Johnson, Jay K., and Samuel O. Brookes. "Benton Points, Turkey Tails and Cache Blades: Middle Archaic exchange in the Midsouth," *Southeastern Archaeology* (1989) 8:134–145.

Smith, Bruce D. "The Archaeology of the Southeastern United States: From Dalton to de Soto, 10,500 BP–500 BP," in *Advances in World Archaeology*, ed. Fred Wendorf and Angela Close. New York: Academic Press, 1986, 5:1–92.

The Emergence of Historic Indian Tribes in the Southeast

Patricia Galloway

Introduction

> *Looked at from the point of view of other organisms, humankind*
> *. . . resembles an acute epidemic disease, whose occasional lapses into*
> *less virulent forms of behavior have never yet sufficed to permit any*
> *really stable, chronic relationship to establish itself.[1]*

The popular notion of Indian[2] tribes' historical emergence has them emerging from the dark of a sort of amorphous prehistory that covers the past of any people whose mode of recording the past cannot now be deciphered, whether it is the prehistory of early man in Olduvai Gorge in Kenya, tens of thousands of years ago, or the prehistory of the Goths exploding into the Roman world in an early century of the present millennium. This is not the kind of emergence I am going to talk about. But the notion of emergence is not a bad one. The reason we have the impression of "emergence" is that we do not know much about how Native Americans lived before the coming of Europeans. Europeans' acquaintance with Native Americans developed as a process over time, by virtue of a simple increase in the quantity of contacts and of documentation of those contacts.

Additionally, Native Americans emerged in a different sense as, struggling with European disease and the new ground rules that Europeans enforced, they changed their cultures to survive. Finally, historical paradigms have changed over the past hundred years, as the history of the everyday life of ordinary people began to emerge and the limelight of political history began to fade.

Native Americans were not prehistoric one day and historic the next as they became known over time to the Europeans who were encroaching on their lands. They have become known more thoroughly over time by improvements in our knowledge of their prehistoric as well as their historic past. Historians have devised the notion of a "protohistoric" period, between the time when the very earliest contacts between European and Native American were made in the sixteenth century and the time when they came into sustained contact with each other in the late seventeenth century. This is the time period during which Native Americans can be said to have "emerged" into the "light" of western history (although of course they had been moving in their own historical light, invisible to us, for millennia). The dramatic changes that took place in Indian cultures in this period will be the centerpiece of the discussion that follows. But first I want to outline the earliest peopling of the Americas and address some basic questions about the encounter between European and Indian.

As Westerners we are all imbued with an ideology that finds "progress" good. It is hard for us not to think that Native American cultures must have been somehow "inferior" to western cultures because they were less advanced technologically at the time of contact. It is worthwhile to look briefly at the reason why this had come to be. Since mankind apparently developed only once and in one place, then in theory everyone started equal. The reason for the discrepancy, the reason indeed why all the problems of the modern world seem to become more and more monumental and complex as time goes on, comes down to a single extremely important factor: population.

Some Canadian Indians refer to themselves as the First Nations, and indeed Indians were the first discoverers of the western hemisphere in a very real sense. *Homo sapiens* did not dwell here at all before Indians crossed the Beringia land bridge during several interglacial time periods ranging from 36,000 to 13,000 years ago. This means that rather than having hundreds of thousands of years to populate the Americas, as mankind had for the rest of the world, these first Americans had at most thirty thousand years to do so. Except in certain very attractive environmental settings they did not become very crowded in the process. Recent reexaminations of the native population of the Americas in 1492 have suggested population levels as high as 100,000,000 (although a more conservative figure of about 70,000,000 may be more realistic). This must be compared with 60–70,000,000 for western Europe alone and 332,000,000 to 542,000,000 for all of the eastern hemisphere.[3] Although the Americas were far from empty when the Europeans arrived, they were not as crowded as the regions from which their invaders came.

Population density plays a very important role in the development of social and political complexity, as the modern growth of government suggests. Though increasing population density is encouraged by a sedentary form of subsistence, the relationship between the two is a synergistic one, because the former also encourages the latter. Furthermore, the feeding of increasing numbers of people on the same land requires a degree of management so as to facilitate the intensification of subsistence activities, and this requirement leads to increasing social complexity.

If population and environment stayed the same, societies would reproduce themselves largely without change, on the assumption that a successful adaptation shouldn't be tampered with. But where population increases, the same subsistence practices will increasingly degrade the environment over time, thus requiring that some change take place if the society is to survive. Better ways to exploit the environment, more efficient ways to distribute food, ways to make the source of subsistence secure, and methods of control of many of these factors must be found. In this way societies change. So far very few human societies have checked population expansion, so it must be taken as a given that all known societies have had to develop better and better ways to get more and more from the environment. But because the Indians had less dense populations than the peoples of Europe, and less dense agglomerations of population to nurture innovation, they had not developed the metallurgy crucial to intensive agriculture except in several particularly dense population centers in Mesoamerica and South America. Furthermore, by evolutionary fluke and extinction, they had no large mammals suitable for augmenting human strength and speed. Finally, because there was still not significant competition for land for subsistence, again except for the two regions cited, they had not yet developed that mother of so much technological invention, total war.

Another important question arises when we compare the Americas to Africa, which was entered and exploited for raw materials during the same period that the Americas were colonized and was drained of its people through the slave trade as well. So why didn't the Americas remain Indian as Africa remained African? For one thing, parts of the Americas, like Mexico and the Andean highlands, did remain significantly Indian, whereas parts of Africa, like the northern region from the Sahara northward, did not remain black. But there are important reasons why black Africa was not as seriously affected by European incursions as was Indian America.

Several significant African kingdoms were as complex as the Aztec and Inca empires of the Americas, they were more populous in general, and they had mastered more kinds of metallurgy than had those American empires. One reason for their advance is that Africa was constantly in touch with both the Middle East, where sedentary civilizations first developed, and with Europe. Africa was also buffeted by the aspirations of those two centers of civilization: its north was conquered first by the Romans and then by the Arabs; its eastern flank was colonized by Arab and Indian traders. It had, in short, been compelled to devise responses to expansionist external influences for a long time and in ways that the Americas were not. In addition, since it was always in touch with these cultures, Africa was also in touch with their diseases, so that the coming of Europeans or Arabs or Hindus did not bring with it swingeing devastation from unknown and irresistible disease.

Because we are part of the European expansion into the rest of the world that brought with it European economic domination, we tend to judge that the European way of life was somehow "better" than that of the peoples who eventually fell under its domination. But there is a less judgmental way to view this process that focuses on its economic aspect. Many scholars see this sequence of events as part of a larger picture, in which the European initiative led to a world system in which Europe became the consuming core that absorbed the raw materials of the non-European periphery, and in the process forced the periphery into dependent status, creating "underdevelopment" where it had not existed before.

This happened to a greater or lesser extent depending on what products of other cultures Europeans desired. If all they wanted was raw materials, then the culture that supplied them had to be made to concentrate upon the production of raw materials: European manufactured goods would be traded in exchange to give natives more time to extract raw materials. In this way many native crafts were lost through neglect as self-sufficient subsistence systems were converted to market economies. Where Europeans were interested in finished goods, the conversion to a market economy was also encouraged, but to the extent that such a conversion conflicted with the preservation of the portion of the culture that produced the desired commodity, it was less successful. Thus North American Indians, from whom Europeans were interested in obtaining only the skins and furs of animals, were urged to amplify production by using firearms, cotton and woolen cloths, metal tools, and metal cooking pots, and in the process bow-hunting skills, the spinning and weaving of bark-fiber cloth, the making of stone tools, and the fabrication of certain kinds of native pottery were abandoned and lost. But China, from which Europeans wished to purchase porcelain, silk fabrics, and jade, retains those crafts at a high level of mastery to this day.

There were of course other factors in this economic equation, including the role government played in any people's social organization and economic system, which in turn was connected with the number of people and their principal subsistence base. Where rulers were powerful and controlled economic activities—and this tended to be true when the most luxurious manufactured goods, which were usually what the Europeans wanted, were of limited circulation controlled by the ruler—then the Europeans could not ultimately dislodge those rulers and had to make use of them as best they could. But where social organization was not so strong or where Europeans were not interested in what the native peoples saw as luxury goods (or were only interested in them as raw materials, as with Inca and Aztec gold), then Europeans could break or negate the power of local rulers by dealing directly with individual native people for raw materials and indeed organizing the production process for their own profit.

But if we are to understand how all these processes took place with reference to the native cultures of the Southeast, we need to know a bit more than just what took place during the meeting of native and European cultures. We need to step back into that shrouded prehistory to discover in a real sense where the Native Americans of the Southeast were coming from.

Corn Mother: The American Neolithic

The son of Kanati (Lucky Hunter) and Selu (Corn) had as his companion a wild boy who had sprung from the blood of a deer killed by Kanati. Making mischief, the boys released all the game Kanati had

*carefully husbanded, making it necessary to hunt. When the boys
wanted food, they often observed Selu going to the provision-house to
bring back corn and beans. One day they spied upon Selu in the
provision-house, and saw that she obtained the corn by rubbing her
stomach and the beans by rubbing under her arms. Thinking that
Selu was a witch, the boys planned to kill her. Selu instructed them to
clear a large piece of ground and drag her body over it seven times.
The boys killed her with clubs and dragged her body over the ground;
where her blood fell corn sprang up. Because the boys only cleared
some small separate areas, corn will not grow everywhere; because they
only dragged her body around twice, Indians only obtain two crops of
corn per year.*

—Cherokee legend[4]

Farming in the eastern hemisphere began with what is referred to as the
"Neolithic revolution," when people first began to domesticate plants and
animals in the Middle East in about 9000–7000 B.C. A similar revolution
took place in the western hemisphere, but it took place later, from about 3000
B.C. in Mesoamerica and 1000 B.C. in North America. The most important
domesticant of the New World was corn, and it was developed over a period of
3000 years from a highland Mesoamerican grass, *teosinte*.[5]

The Eastern Woodlands of North America offered a very rich environment
for hunters and gatherers, as early Euro-american pioneers west of the Appalachians quickly found before they had time to clear land and make their first
crop. Before commercial hunting of deer began at the end of the seventeenth
century, white-tailed deer were everywhere in plenty. Fat turkeys roosted in the
trees and enormous flocks of waterfowl and passenger pigeons migrated
through the region every year. The wide meandering rivers and the lakes
formed by their old beds were full of fish, as were the coastal waters. Fruit and
nut trees and thickets full of berries were plentiful, and wild grapevines fes-
tooned the forests. Compared to the marginal environments where the only
remaining hunter-gatherers now live on less than six hours of work a day, the
Eastern Woodlands and especially the Southeast represented a paradise of ease
for hunter-gatherers. They developed what archaeologists refer to as "Primary
Forest Efficiency," making full use of the complete range of these resources.
They were well fed and prosperous, and their populations grew rapidly.

Hunter-gatherers do not simply wander around aimlessly; they limit themselves to a seasonal round of specific places and activities so as to make op-
timum use of their environment while minimizing their requirements for

traveling. Over time, hunter-gatherer groups in the Southeast tended to establish within a single familiar territory an area where they spent more time and were able to cache some possessions and food, a base camp. This camp might be well-located to serve for a long sojourn during the winter months, for example, and over time old people or pregnant women might be left there for longer and longer periods of time.

Among the foods gathered by these people were oily and starchy seeds like chenopodium (lamb's-quarters) and amaranth. As had happened in the Middle Eastern "cradle of civilization," over time the people began to plant some of the best of these seeds and to return to harvest the crop they had thus encouraged, just as they returned to a good bramble thicket at berry time each year. When contacts to the Mesoamerican south made early maize varieties available, the woodland peoples were already prepared to take an interest in planting it. Perhaps the earliest planters of corn on a significant basis were the peoples of the Lower Mississippi Valley who made up what archaeologists call the Coles Creek culture, beginning in A.D. 600–700. Although little corn has been found on Coles Creek sites, there has been some, and the Coles Creek peoples also built ceremonial centers characterized by mounds built to support temples, centers where only a small population lived.

But the most impressive cultural remains built on a corn subsistence base in eastern North America were those of the Mississippian peoples of the great central Mississippi Valley, whose cultural influence was felt across the whole southeastern region. This culture, which developed after about A.D. 800, was supported by the cultivation of Northern Flint corn, whose short growing season made corn cultivation practicable in the Midwest and further north for the first time.

This great flourishing of culture in the heartland of North America was no accident: it was predicated upon the presence of enormously rich river valley soils. The American Bottom region around Saint Louis was as rich in river alluvium as the storied Nile delta, annually renewed not only by soils washed down by the Mississippi's northern tributaries, but also by the enormous Missouri-Platte system draining the whole of the northern Great Plains. It was rich soil, never before cultivated. Such alluvial soil is light and easily cultivable with the digging sticks and simple hoes the people had to use. Because the great Mississippi River system during its long history had created a multitude of lakes, the people were able to add protein to their diets with the fish in those lakes and the waterfowl that traveled north and south along the river every year to eat the fish. They probably worked harder as farmers than they had as hunter-gatherers, but they were able to support more people on the same land and their health and life expectancy improved.

It used to be believed that the whole phenomenon of Mississippian culture and maize agriculture in the eastern woodlands could be simply explained in terms of Mesoamerican missionaries and a great evangelizing center at Cahokia in the American Bottom, whose missionaries carried bags of seed corn. Archaeological research has shown over the years that this is not a true picture. Widespread trading and communication networks all over North America meant that corn was probably available to almost everyone who wanted it at virtually the same time, and where broad floodplains suited to its cultivation were available, there people cultivated it. So there are important centers of Mississippian culture to be found across the Southeast, from Spiro in eastern Oklahoma to Etowah in Georgia, each as individual in its cultural texture as environmental variation across the region might suggest. Two important areas of Mississippian activity toward the center of the region are the Black Warrior River in Alabama, which supported the Moundville center with its tributary sites, and the Yazoo-Mississippi delta, an even richer habitat than the American Bottom, where numerous Mississippian centers developed. Further down the Mississippi, in the Natchez Bluffs region, the Coles Creek pioneers continued to develop their own mound-building culture, called Plaquemine by archaeologists.

Choosing a Chief: Development of Ranked Societies

> *The first man created on earth called the other people together and told them that they should choose one man, abler and wiser than any other man among them, to be their chief, and that whatever the chief should command should be done by the people, who would look on him as a great father. The people held a council and chose this powerful first man, and Coyote told them they should call him Moon because he was first created.*
>
> —*Caddo legend*[6]

Mississippian societies did not just happen overnight, and people did not just settle down on the land as happy egalitarian farmers to grow corn. As we have seen, there are important environmental requirements for the successful cultivation of corn. With wood and stone technology a light and friable soil is needed, and because corn quickly exhausts the fertility of the land on which it is planted, some means of renewing it will help avoid the necessity for the constant clearing of new land. Significant river floodplains are the answer to these problems, for floods bring natural renewal of fertility and flood-deposited soils are easy to work without animal traction power. Because corn is not a complete food, it needs to be supplemented with proteins from both plant and animal sources, which means that semisedentary southeastern hunter-gatherers would need to retain a portion of their repertoire of exploitation techniques. Because they could not afford to go very far away and still attend to their fields, it was advantageous that they choose locations for those fields that were convenient to a variety of wild foodstuffs. For this reason Mississippian settlement tended to favor not only broad floodplains, but floodplains that were located favorably with respect to the borders of several ecological zones, giving the inhabitants relatively convenient access to all their subsistence needs.

These preferences had the effect of narrowing the available choice of land. In the early days of Mississippian agriculture this may not have been a problem at all, because agricultural productivity was so dramatically greater than the efficiency of gathering that it was possible to support many more people than there actually were on the available optimal lands. Once again, however, population drove change.

As population increases to the point that it strains the carrying capacity of the land, subsistence methods must be changed or must become more efficient. For Mississippian agriculture to become more efficient it needed to be better organized. Someone had to keep track of planting times; someone had to see that seed corn and surpluses were carefully kept against need. Where help was needed with planting or harvest, that help had to be in the right place at the right time. Where everything the settlement needed was not directly available to it, someone had to organize trade or redistribution to acquire what was needed. These tasks and probably many more fell under the purview of Mississippian chiefs.

Kinship was the base on which the power of chiefs rested. As hunter-gatherers had settled down to become part-time and then full-time farmers, their leaders were the leaders of lineages and clans. Over time different lineages and clans that controlled different resources or that were more successful in building alliances with their neighbors emerged to hold positions of influence and responsibility. Their leaders were men, but especially because of the continuance of seasonal hunting instead of stockraising, women dominated the holding of land by staying at home on it most of the time and by being the bearers of the lineages and the householders; Mississippian societies seem to have traced kinship predominantly through the female line and to have sent men to live in their wives' households.

Chiefs kept their positions by making sure that the most influential among their followers were satisfied, over and above the organizing tasks the chiefs carried out. Leaders were praised not for being rich but for being generous; it was a chiefly virtue to be able to give things to followers over which only the chief had control. In some instances these things were elaborate and time-consuming craft items controlled by the chief's support of the craftsman. In other instances such items might be acquired through long-distance trade monopolized by the chief as he used local products to trade for exotic items.

We do not know the details of Mississippian chiefly power or all of its sources, but archaeology provides us with the evidence for its trappings, and that evidence suggests that Mississippian chiefs probably carried out priestly functions connected with worship of the sun—so necessary to the success of agricultural crops—and with fertility and death. This power was significant, because it was able to organize the labor to build the great flat-topped mounds of the Mississippian center, mounds which were used to support temple struc-tures and thereby to reach a little nearer the sun, but whose construction provided no immediate tangible benefit to the people who built it.

Some Mississippian chiefs were able to add to their power over time as successful settlements grew and expanded and eventually spawned daughter settlements, so that eventually the chief of a successful settlement would find himself the paramount of a group of settlements. If he continued to be success-ful at the tasks that made his people prosperous, the daughter settlements would also prosper and have daughters themselves, or through marriage al-liances with neighbors he might add another settlement to his group. The leaders of important paramount centers like Cahokia, Moundville, and Win-terville at their respective peaks were important men, with trading contacts all over the Southeast and beyond.

But Mississippian societies weren't immortal. Intensification of agricultural techniques could only go so far in the absence of a significant technological advance, and eventually it would be difficult to maintain large population concentrations around the same center as soil exhaustion permeated all the nearby lands and game and firewood became depleted. It would be possible to fallow nearby fields and to move to fields farther and farther away, but under

This disc is perhaps the best known artifact excavated at the Moundville site in Alabama. The sandstone disc depicts a rattlesnake motif surrounding the hand and eye engraved in the center. Photograph by Chip Cooper.

those conditions the time would come when "the center could not hold." At that point either centralized organization would have to break down completely or some degree of decentralization would have to take place.

Exhaustion of the land was not the only hazard. Hierarchical chiefdom organization is expensive, and as people made settlements at greater distances and looked toward a more modest local center, they might begin to wonder why they needed a paramount chief at all. It might become harder to collect the tribute required to maintain the ceremonial center. When daughter villages split away from the paramount, junior branches of the chiefly lineage might try to make the split permanent, and they might succeed.

Events beyond the chief's control might also affect him; if the external trading partners who provided him with the exotic goods he used to impress his constituents should cut off communication for any reason, whether they themselves were in trouble or warfare had closed trade routes, the chief might find it hard to hold his supporters together. A series of crop failures, perhaps implying loss of favor with the supernatural or predictive failure on the chief's part, could also undermine his power. Finally, as suitable lands filled up, more successful neighbors might undertake warfare to annex outlying villages or to gain domination over important hunting grounds.

Thus Mississippian societies were continually evolving and changing and cannot be thought of as set in a kind of eternal stasis. When Europeans arrived at the turn of the sixteenth century, the Mississippian societies of the Southeast were in various stages of this continuous change, and at least at first the newcomers merely represented another problem to be dealt with.

Some of the Mississippian chiefdoms had fallen apart. That had been the fate of the greatest and earliest of them, Cahokia, for its people had dispersed into more modest settlements in the Midwest by 1350. Moundville was in a debilitated state, for although people still lived in large numbers in some of the peripheral settlements of the chiefdom, it is likely that Moundville itself had been abandoned by 1500. Other chiefdoms were functioning well in the region. The great Plaquemine site at Emerald was the seat of a paramount who dominated numerous settlements in the Natchez Bluffs region, while the Haynes Bluff site on the lower Yazoo had influence through the lower Yazoo Basin. None of these people were expecting anything other than that they would continue to cope with problems much like those they had seen before, and that the corn mother and the eagle dancer would sustain and protect them.

The Long Migration: Disruptions of the First Encounters

The Choctaws emigrated from a land far in the west, following the Creeks and Chickasaws. They were led by a great prophet who carried with him a long white pole as the badge of his authority. When he planted it straight up in the earth, that was the signal for making camp; while they were in camp, the pole altered its position, inclining toward the rising of the sun. This was the signal for the Choctaws to proceed on their journey. The pole continued to incline toward the east until they reached Nanih Waiya, where it remained perpendicular. From this they concluded that they had found the land in which they were to settle.

-Choctaw legend[7]

The encounter of the eastern and western hemispheres beginning at the end of the fifteenth century has been seen as a reunion of the human family, a rejoining of two "Old Worlds" after millennia of separation. This would indeed be something to celebrate if the meeting had not had such tragic consequences,

Nanih Waiya, the great mound and ceremonial center for the Choctaw, is located in Winston County. Photograph courtesy of Mississippi Department of Archives and History.

leading to the nearly complete destruction of the pre-Columbian cultures of the Americas. The destruction of cultures was not always complete nor always intentional, but it nevertheless meant that the historic tribes of the Southeast, like all Indian groups in the hemisphere, were the product of an encounter that altered their ways of life profoundly from what they had been before.

In those early encounters there was a striking inequity. The conquistadors of Iberia were not men of the princely families of Europe, but were instead mostly disinherited younger sons, soldiers of fortune who with the closing of the Spanish frontier on the expulsion of the Moors in 1492 faced a loss of opportunity for gaining lands and fortune by the sword. The "discovery" of a "New World" and the claims made on its souls by the Roman Catholic church gave them a new crusade to fight, a crusade that promised fabulous riches as well as the garnering of souls for the church. Although the vigorous campaigning of Bartolomé de Las Casas, the famous "defender of the Indians" whose criticism of Spanish cruelty created the so-called "Black Legend," led to a

Right: Bartolomé de Las Casas, engraving (*Narrative and Critical History of America, II, Spanish Explorations and Settlements in America from the Fifteenth to the Seventeenth Century*), (Boston: Houghton Mifflin, 1889) from the portrait by A. Lara in the Biblioteca Capitular Colombina, Seville. *Bottom:* The depictions by Theodore de Bry of Spanish brutality to the Indians were widely disseminated. Courtesy of Mississippi Department of Archives and History.

Early eighteenth-century engraving showing the chief of Coosa coming to greet Soto and his army. Photograph courtesy of Mississippi Department of Archives and History.

modification of Spanish policy in 1542 and a lengthy discussion of the status of Indians as free people in the 1550s, such was not the attitude of the conquerors, who believed that they were dealing with savages whose status as such made conquest and exploitation by any means permissible.

The chiefs of the American peoples met by the conquistadors, on the other hand, were often hereditary rulers, and their leading men the equivalent of royal councillors. Theirs was, at least in the initial encounter, an entirely different attitude. The Indian peoples by and large attempted to receive the Iberians as they would receive a foreign embassy sent by a distant, unknown, and possibly inferior people. There was no attempt to change them in any way, even though many of the peoples of the Americas saw them as uncivilized and uncouth.

Much has been made of the debilitating effects of the native belief that the Iberians were gods. The first such instance cited was the Arawak reaction to Columbus. The Italian noted in his log that the Indians thought the Europeans had come from Heaven. How Columbus could have known that is nothing short of miraculous in itself, but is a very convenient argument for the rightness of subjugating them. There is less doubt about the Aztec belief that the fair-skinned god Quetzalcoatl would return from the east, for we know they had that belief, but it was smallpox rather than the fear of Quetzalcoatl that laid the Aztec empire low. Certainly the peoples of the Southeast thought much less of Hernando de Soto: the chief of the mighty chiefdom of Quigualtam, when told that the Spanish leader claimed to be a child of the sun and demanded that he appear to make obeisance, responded imperiously that if Soto was indeed a child of the sun, he should dry up the Mississippi to prove it.

The meeting of these two groups was bound to end badly for one of them. The Europeans were seriously overmatched everywhere, especially in the Southeast, and only very seldom did they undertake pitched battles with the natives, in spite of the advantage their horses provided in open country. Still, when fighting did take place, it had very different effects on either side, related to the style of fighting both used. The Spaniards had cavalry and footsoldiers, chain mail, swords, lances, crossbows, and primitive firearms; and the Spaniards killed in the mass, wherever they could corner a mass of people (as Soto did in the ponds of Apalachee and in the walled town of Mabila). None of the Indians of the Americas had metal edged weapons, and southeastern Indians had little more than clubs and lances and arrows tipped with stone or sharpened antler; and although the Indians were deadly accurate with their bows, they fought a guerrilla war of annoyance, not mass murder. The cumulative effect of these two technical panoplies and fighting styles, therefore, was that the Europeans killed more people than the Indians did, even though they were vastly outnumbered.

We have already seen that the peoples of the Southeast had become agriculturists by the time of the encounter and were living in large nucleated groups scattered across the major river floodplains of the region. Chiefdom societies, with their centralized communication and administration, were ideal breeding grounds for the crowd diseases of Europe and the eastern hemisphere, diseases like smallpox, measles, diphtheria, cholera, yellow fever, plague. These diseases required carriers in great enough numbers and in robust enough health not to die before passing them on. These requirements were met in the Europeans and Africans who came to the Americas.

Because the eastern hemisphere's diseases had been lost entirely or attenuated greatly by the arduous crossing of the arctic regions as people first entered

Soto discovers the Mississippi River, 5 May 1541. This large oil painting hangs in the State Historical Museum in Jackson, Mississippi. Photograph courtesy of Mississippi Department of Archives and History.

Archaeologists think that these three sixteenth-century Spanish bells found near Clarksdale, Mississippi, came to that area with the Hernando de Soto expedition in 1541. The bells are on display at the Winterville Mound Museum near Greenville, Mississippi. Photograph courtesy of Mississippi Department of Archives and History.

the western hemisphere, Indians there were all susceptible to the European diseases, and given uniform exposure, the numbers of deaths were limited only by genetic peculiarities and the viability of the germ. Exposures were not uniform, of course; some diseases were passed from populations that had encountered Europeans to those that had not, but because the diseases killed off the contacted populations so rapidly, the effects of diseases reaching the interior in that way were much muted. For that reason the interior Southeast was not completely devastated by the time Hernando de Soto crossed it in 1539–42, even though ships had been mooring on its coasts and its chiefs had been trading for the products of affected areas for at least some twenty years.

The direct contact of conquest expeditions like those of Panfilo de Narváez or Hernando de Soto was another potential source of disease exposure, though here the exposure was limited to the kinds of chronic diseases that men and animals could carry without being killed by them. The overall effect was that although disease exposure led to horrifying mortality among American natives, in the Southeast the worst of this was seen on the coastal plain and piedmont, while the interior was not so seriously affected.

Where there had been serious mortality, the effects on native societies were devastating. When leaders and old people died, all that survived about how the society was supposed to work was the more modest knowledge of domestic routine that everyone knew. When so many died that crops could not be planted, fruits not gathered, and game not hunted, people starved to death. To keep on living, the survivors tried to reconstruct their societies by joining together to create new settlements approximating the old ones they knew.

The result of this urge to restore the world to its proper working order in the Southeast was a series of population movements and amalgamations. Peoples who had not been badly affected by disease mortality, whose societies were still relatively intact, might take in people with whom they had had marriage alliances before, and assimilation accordingly took place. Such was the case with the Natchez, inheritors of the Plaquemine culture, who took in smaller remnants of the Tunican Grigras, Tioux, and Coroas. Where smaller groups of people came together, none of them populous enough to recreate a proper society, but many partly intact and distinctive in culture, confederacies might be constructed in which the constituent groups retained a modicum of autonomy: such was the case with the Choctaws and the upper and lower Creek confederacies.

One overlooked European disease carrier in the southeast: Soto's pigs! Courtesy of Mississippi Department of Archives and History.

Rabbit Trickster: Brokers and the Playoff System

Wildcat was always catching and eating young rabbits, so that none of them grew up. One day Rabbit went to Wildcat and told him he knew of a plan by which Wildcat could get some turkeys to eat. He told him to lie down and play dead. Then he went to the turkeys and told them he had killed Wildcat and invited them to come and dance around the body while he sang for them. So the turkeys went with him and began to dance around Wildcat as Rabbit sang, "catch that big red-legged one" or "catch the biggest one." Thinking that Rabbit was joking, they danced ever more carelessly, until Wildcat jumped up and caught the biggest gobbler. Rabbit thus made Wildcat his friend, and the turkey learned to peer carefully at everything.
—Hitchiti legend[8]

The loss of the "high" cultures of the Americas through the ravages of European disease was bad enough, but more was to come; the American natives only began to walk upon the European historical stage when they came into constant contact with Europeans, and that same contact changed their societies further.

The peoples of the Southeast were lucky, because they had no resources valuable enough to justify the investment in supervision required for the implementation of slave labor, as was the case with the gold and silver of Hispaniola, Mexico, and Peru. At first, indeed, the Spaniards were forced to admit that all the southeastern Indians had was land very favorable for the raising of cattle. So when Spaniards formed settlements in Florida with the intention of protecting and harboring the treasure fleets, cattle were brought and eventually ranched in northern Florida. But in the early seventeenth century, before cattle could be established, there was need for dried meat for the provisioning of ships bound for Spain, and the Indians of the interior—future Creeks, their tribal names still echoing those Soto heard—began to hunt the plentiful deer for this trade, obtaining for their dried meat bright cloth, glittering brass ornaments, and perhaps even guns.

The southeastern peoples continued lucky through the seventeenth and eighteenth centuries. Although the colonial powers began to struggle for nominal control of the region with the establishment of Jamestown in 1607, St. Marks in 1633, Charles Towne in 1670, Pensacola in 1698, and Mobile in 1700, not one of them was committed to a significant transplantation of colonial population or to complete domination and assimilation of the Indians. The Spaniards, although committed to a mission system, remained too few in number and were limited to the peninsula of Florida by British destruction of their missions by 1704; the British entrusted activities in the interior to capitalist traders, who jealously guarded their private alliances with chiefs; and the French, always too few in number to repudiate the ideal of the Noble Savage, were constrained by a mercantilist policy that forbade the export of finished goods from the Louisiana colony.

Thus, except for a short period at the beginning of the eighteenth century when men from Carolina thought a profit could be made in Indian slaves, the most important product of the Southeast as far as Europe was concerned became the one raw material that had a profitable market in Europe: the product of the hunt, which Indians were much more proficient in obtaining then European colonists would be. Indians were willing to provide this product because the Europeans were able to capitalize on a differential view of value.

To southeastern Indians, deerskins were the easiest thing in the world to obtain, and any man who was physically capable could obtain them; they were not therefore valuable in the native scheme of things, nor had they been so viewed prior to the coming of Europeans. To Europeans, witnessing the beginning of an industrial explosion that would revolutionize labor in Europe, the manufactured goods they traded to the Indians were cheap and gaudy rubbish, making the acquisition of deerskins very profitable indeed. But to the natives ready-made cloth meant a drastic reduction in labor costs for clothing, while metal tools completely revolutionized the tasks of agriculture. Furthermore, when a man was motivated to kill many deer, his family could eat better than ever before. The Europeans, on the other hand, supplied deerskin to the clothing industry and to other industrial applications; it was not so subject to fad as the beaver pelts of the north. Apparently, everyone was a winner in this trade.

Everyone, that is, except the chiefs who were not able to control this source of exotic prestige goods. Europeans made their own lives easier by giving a nod to the remaining Indian power structures as they periodically presented special gifts of fancy goods such as silver jewelry and dress uniform coats to the chiefs. But they were quick to realize that they could manipulate those power structures by giving supplies of gifts to certain men who favored their plans, and those men in turn would use the gifts to build factions favorable to the desired European objective. It must be admitted, however, that the persistent failure of Europeans to understand the ethics and kinship loyalties of the southeastern tribes made such policies far less effective than they could have been. Indeed, since there was no shortage of astute native leaders, the Europeans soon found this strategy turned back upon them as they were caught in the clutches of what one scholar has called a "play-off system," whereby they were played off against one another as tribes learned to manipulate prices by never giving entire allegiance to any European power.

In this way, by forcing the Europeans to fit into their own systems of alliance, southeastern Indians were able to take some control of the direction in which their societies would evolve. Thus the Natchez, fed up with French encroachment on traditional sacred sites, revolted and killed most of the men at French Fort Rosalie in 1729. When the French retaliated by sending some into slavery in Santo Domingo and driving the rest off their lands, the Natchez took refuge among the Chickasaws, whose laws of hospitality meant that even two French wars, both unsuccessful, could not force the relinquishment of the refugees. Thus the Alabamas profited from the presence of both an English trading house and a French fort on their lands, which marked a border between French and English interests. In spite of a stereotyped notion of "client warfare" popular in Eurocentric history texts, the fact is that southeastern native peoples allied with Europeans and traded with Europeans, but they almost never did much damage on behalf of Europeans.

That is not to say that European issues and events did not give them cause to do damage to one another on their own behalf. The process of building tribal identities out of demographic wreckage, added to the new economic context created by European trade, created a complex situation in which new leaders with a grasp of these new conditions, leaders perhaps from lineages never prominent before, had a chance to emerge. Often these leaders were people of the kind characterized by anthropologists as "cultural brokers," people who were knowledgeable about but not successful in their own culture, who understood how to use the opportunities represented by the European contact to build factional power. In the beginning these people were entirely Indian, men with some pretension to power who were able to build on it with European resources like the Choctaw chief Red Shoe or the Creek Wolf King, or women like Mary Bosomworth who married European traders and learned to manage their husbands for the benefit of their people. Leaders like these took their tribes in new directions that often required negotiating the pitfalls of a playoff system that could lead to the danger of civil war. In doing so they placed more strain on such deeply-rooted traditions as blood revenge and fictive kinship alliances.

As time went on, the native matrilineal kinship system allowed the children of French interpreters and British traders and their Indian wives to become the living image of the intermediary. When the balance of population and actual military dominance began to shift in favor of the Euro-Americans, which did not happen until a single "American" power emerged from the imperial struggles of the eighteenth century, these mixed-bloods were well-placed in positions of influence to draw on both loyalties and influence changes in their societies profoundly.

Postscript: The Civilized Tribes' Reward

> *A Creek chief died. When the chief was dead he appeared before Gohantone, who said to him, "This land belongs to you and your children forever. This land will be yours forever, but these whites who have just come will overwhelm you and inherit your land. They will increase and the Indian will decrease and at last die out. Then only white people will remain. But there will be terrible times."*
> *—Yuchi legend[9]*

The triumph of the British over the French in the Seven Years' War in 1763 was shortlived. They were replaced by the Americans in 1783 and 1815, which made an end of the Indians' options and initiated another period of dramatic cultural change. Before the Americans took over, southeastern Indians of the interior controlled their lands and could not be threatened or driven off them, since behind the Indians lay another European power. Surrounded now by Americans, or at least uniformly pushed by them from the east, Indians were at the mercy of American policies.

Those policies were not long in evolving, first to encompass assimilation, turning Indians into industrious peasant farmers under the tutelage of missionaries who would teach them to read and write and would expunge their savage habits. The fact that the deerskin trade of the eighteenth century had begun to deplete the deer population made it easier for the missionaries to urge the conversion to farming, but they were not particularly successful in persuading the men to undertake a task that had been assigned to women from the beginning of agricultural sedentism in the region. Instead, much to the chagrin of the missionaries, the men began to stay longer away from home as they turned to more distant regions for game. Missionaries were stringent in stamping out overt evidences of savagery like the pre-burial scaffolding of corpses. They enlisted the laws of the new territories and states to help stamp out the immoral practices of matrilineal kinship, which they viewed as irresponsible behavior on the part of a child's genetic father when he left the support of his children to their mother's kin. Building mission schools, they began the practice of separating the children from their Indian homes to enculturate them fully to the lower echelon of white society for which they deemed them fitted.

Many Indians of the Southeast wished to adopt features of white society and to assimilate. The so-called Five Civilized Tribes—Cherokee, Chickasaw, Choctaw, Creek, and Seminole—did in fact learn many of these new ways: the Cherokees copied the new American form of government and even created their own alphabet and newspaper; some of the Choctaws would eventually own black slaves. But none of this was enough when population pressures in the old Anglo settlements east of the Appalachians created a public demand for Indian land. Ol' Hickory himself speculated in Creek lands before he engineered the Creek Wars, pitting progressives against the traditional Red Sticks who had no desire to assimilate, and he made participation in the war on the American side a litmus test for the Civilized Tribes. But nothing would be good enough as long as Indian lands lay fertile and broad before Americans now grasping for cotton and tobacco lands to feed a full-blown Industrial Revolution. In the end all their efforts to assimilate were set at naught. The payment the Five Civilized Tribes received for saving the day at the Battle of New Orleans and helping win the Creek Wars was Removal west of the Mississippi, which started with the deportation of the Choctaws in 1830.

NOTES

1. William McNeill, *Plagues and Peoples* (New York: Anchor, 1977), 20.

2. The term "Indian" of course stems from Columbus's mistake in thinking he had reached the East Indies, but most Native Americans now use this less cumbersome term to refer to themselves collectively, and I will use it here in that sense.

3. Russell Thornton, *American Indian Holocaust and Survival: A Population History Since 1492* (Norman: University of Oklahoma Press, 1987), 36–37.

4. Paraphrased from George E. Lankford, *Native American Legends* (1987), 148–151.

5. Marvin Harris, *Culture, People, Nature* (New York: Thomas Y. Crowell, 1975), 212–215, 222–223.

6. Paraphrased from Lankford, *Native American Legends*, 64.

7. Paraphrased from John R. Swanton, *Source Material for the Social and Ceremonial Life of the Choctaw Indians* (BAE Bulletin 103, 1931), 11.

8. Paraphrased from John R. Swanton, *Myths and Tales of the Southeastern Indians* (BAE Report 88, 1929), 47.

9. Paraphrased from Lankford, *Native American Legends*, 137.

SUGGESTED READINGS

Crosby, Alfred W. *Ecological Imperialism: The Biological Expansion of Europe, 900–1900.* Cambridge: Cambridge University Press, 1986.

Hudson, Charles. *The Southeastern Indians.* Knoxville: University of Tennessee Press, 1976.

Milanich, Jerald T., and Milbrath, Susan, (eds.), *First Encounters: Spanish Explorations in the Caribbean and the United States, 1492–1570.* Gainesville: University Presses of Florida, 1989.

Lankford, George E. *Native American Legends.* Little Rock: Harvest House, 1987.

Thornton, Russell. *American Indian Holocaust and Survival: A Population History since 1492.* Norman: University of Oklahoma Press, 1987.

Trail of Treaties
The Choctaws
from the American Revolution
to Removal

Samuel J. Wells[1]

The United States government's relations with the Choctaw Indians from the end of the American Revolution to the Removal of the Indians from·their ancestral homeland can be traced through a series of treaties beginning with the Treaty of Hopewell in 1786 and ending with the Treaty of Dancing Rabbit Creek in 1830.

The first treaty the new American republic made with the Choctaws was a clear signal of attitude and intent. With hindsight much of the language seems arrogant, self-righteous, and hypocritical. The United States decreed that the Choctaws were to stop their practice of *lex talionis* (blood for blood retaliation), return any United States citizens who might be captive in their country, return runaway black slaves to their owners, return any property that might have been taken from United States citizens during the war, and turn Indians who committed crimes against United States citizens over to the American government for prosecution, as well as other provisions. The document ignored the facts that Choctaw country was encompassed by land claimed and occupied by Spain, a nation that also considered the Choctaws under their dominion, and that the Choctaw nation had not actively participated in the

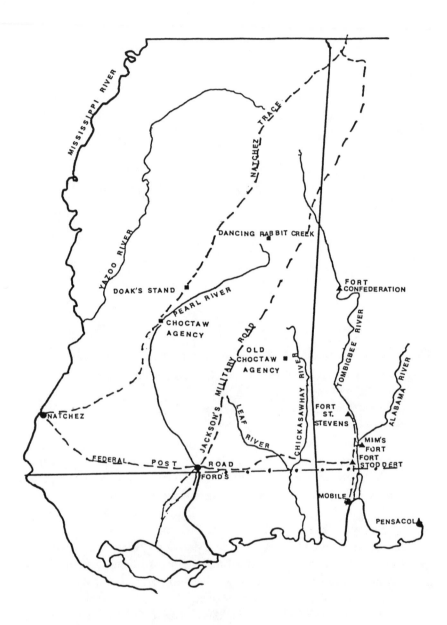

Roads and rivers through Choctaw Country. Courtesy of S. J. Wells.

colonial war. Passive allies of Great Britain primarily because of the British stranglehold on the native economy, the Choctaws would have preferred not to be involved in the white man's conflict at all. Yet in the Treaty of Hopewell, signed in South Carolina on January 3, 1786, the new Americans "granted" the Choctaw nation peace and defined the boundaries of the nation within what the United States government considered American territory. But the international aspects of the treaty could not be dismissed so easily.

Great Britain had not surrendered her desire to possess the Mississippi River Valley when she granted her thirteen American colonies their independence. Her plans to stir up trouble in the region were obvious in the aftermath of the 1783 Treaty of Paris. The British ministers made separate treaties with the United States and the American ally Spain on the same day in 1783. In the treaty with the United States, the southern boundary of British territory being surrendered was the thirty-first parallel. In the treaty with Spain the boundary had not been specifically named, but since the British had so adamantly declared the mouth of the Yazoo (at 32° 26' north) the boundary of West Florida in 1764, the Spanish felt justified in claiming that boundary. The United States and Spain would not settle on the thirty-first parallel as the southern boundary of the United States and the northern boundary of Spanish West Florida until 1795, at San Lorenzo de Real in Madrid; the United States would officially take possession of the region in 1798, but in the meantime relations between the former allies became severely strained and the Choctaws had to test their own diplomatic skills by dealing with both nations.

Both the Spaniards and the Americans treated the Indians paternalistically and tried to exploit tribal members. The Choctaw nation was a loose confederation of about fifty villages with no firm, unified central government. Divided into three sections, sometimes called the Eastern, Western, and Six-town districts, each village acted so independently of the confederation that extraordinary amounts of time and patience were necessary to negotiate treaties with which the majority of Choctaws agreed. Sometimes the white men did not trouble themselves with the formalities. The Spaniards built Fort Nogales at the Walnut Hills (now Vicksburg) without Choctaw permission and only gained a cession for the site after the fact. With their economy now largely dependent on the skin and pelt trade (the raw goods Europeans converted into a myriad of leather products) and their land overhunted, the Indians were forced to cross the Mississippi to seek game. Successive years of drought crippled their agricultural endeavors. Yet when the Grand Chief Franchimastabe reported the problems of his people, the Spanish governor Gayoso declared him an "old rascal" and scoundrel who had nothing more on his mind than exhorting "gifts." The American government sent enticing messages inviting young warriors to come join the American army to learn the military arts so they could better protect their people. The Choctaws called the Americans "Georgians" or "Virginians," and from the conduct of the frontiersmen who acted independently of the United States government the Indians gained a very unfavorable impression of the men who nurtured greed and violence while waiting to claim the Choctaw homeland for their own. In the eyes of these frontiersmen, the Choctaws were a defeated people in a conquered land due to their former alliance with Britain.

The American government finally started putting the Treaty of Hopewell into effect in 1798 when the Spaniards evacuated to south of the thirty-first parallel. Now the United States government regulated trade and licensed the traders. A factory system was instituted. "Factories" were government stocked and staffed trading houses. But the Indians still often dealt with traders from the British firm of Panton and Leslie operating out of Spanish-occupied Pensacola.

On December 17, 1801, the Treaty of Fort Adams reconfirmed the Treaty of Hopewell and provided that a wagon road (which would become known as the Natchez Trace) be made through the Choctaw country and beyond, to have a western boundary of Choctaw country marked east of the Mississippi and to give all the land between the boundary and the river to the United States. Any white settlers in Indian country were to be removed. The Indians received $2000 in goods and merchandise and a promise of three sets of blacksmith tools. The United States received 2,641,920 acres of land.

Benjamin Hawkins, the southeastern Indian agent appointed earlier by President Washington, signed both the Hopewell and Fort Adams treaties for the United States. The signees for the Choctaws varied. Yockonahoma, Yockehoopoie, Mingo Hoopoie, Tobocoh and Pooshemastubie were the principal Choctaws signing the Hopewell treaty.[2] The Treaty of Fort Adams carries the signatures of sixteen Choctaws, but unlike the earlier treaty it does not name the principal men of the nation at the beginning. They are referred to collectively as "mingos, principal men and warriors," though the names of the negotiators for the United States continued to be mentioned by name. In the introductory paragraphs of treaties, only the Treaty of Hopewell names the principals of the Choctaw nation negotiating the treaty. With the Treaty of

Fort Adams a milestone in dealing with the Choctaws was reached. The United States government officials no longer believed it necessary to identify the leading men of the nation by name.

The United States Congress enacted the Trade and Intercourse Act in 1802. It strengthened the factory system and made Choctaw dealings with traders unlicensed by the United States illegal.

The treaty signed on October 17, 1802, at Fort Confederation on the Tombigbee River in Choctaw country authorized anew the marking and redefining of the boundaries, from the Chickasawhay River to the Tombigbee to the bluff of Hach-a-tig-geby. For one dollar the Choctaws agreed to "quit claim" the territory south of this line to the United States boundary. Also, the boundary line near the mouth of the Yazoo River was to be redrawn "as be found convenient." Silas Dinsmoor, United States agent to the Choctaws, and John Pitchlynn and Turner Brashears, both United States government interpreters, witnessed the signatures of Tuskona Hoopoia, Mingo Pooskoos I, Mingo Pooskoos II, and Pushmataha on behalf of the lower towns and Chickasawhay; Oak Chummy and Tuskee Maiab on behalf of the upper towns; Latalahomah, Mooklahoosooieh, Mingo Hom Astubby and Tuskahomah on behalf of the six towns and lower town.

The Treaty of 1803, also known as the Treaty of Hoe Buckintoopa, further detailed agreements reached in the Fort Confederation Treaty and named land ceded to the United States between the Pascagoula, Tombigbee, and Mobile rivers to the Sintee Bogue which amounted to 853,760 acres. Payment given to the Choctaws living along the Tombigbee next to the Sintee Bogue included fifteen blankets, 250 pounds of lead, one bridle, one man's saddle, and one black silk handkerchief.

The Treaty of Mount Dexter, signed in 1805, allotted $48,000 to be applied towards the payment of debts the Choctaws owed traders, and for depredations to stock and other property attributed to the Indians. The interpreter John Pitchlynn, who resided in the Choctaw nation, received $2500 as compensation for personal "losses." The Choctaw nation would receive $3000 worth of goods and merchandise each year plus one-time payments of $500 to each of the three division chiefs, Puckshunubbee-Mingo, Hoomastubee and Pushmataha, who would also receive pensions of $150 per year in return for 4,142,720 acres of land and other concessions such as rights of way for roads through Choctaw country.

The Louisiana Purchase of 1803, in which the United States government gained possession of all French territory west of the Mississippi, as well as New Orleans, did not ease the Americans' growing pains nor lessen their fears of "foreign" influence among the Indians. These fears led the United States to claim by proclamation the Gulf coast area south of the Mississippi territory border in 1810. Spain had secretly returned Louisiana to France prior to the Louisiana Purchase, but did not surrender claim to the Gulf area until the Florida Purchase Treaty (Adams-Onis) in 1819. The British traders operating out of Pensacola, still dealing with the Indians, especially the Creeks located to the east of Choctaw country, were credited, along with the Shawnee Tecumseh and his pan-Indian movement, with stirring up trouble and causing the Creek War of 1813. The war was actually just one front of the War of 1812, where Britain's contempt for her former colonies erupted into bloody violence. This time the Choctaws allied with the Americans.

In the Creek War, the Choctaws found an outlet for old grievances against the Creeks, another loose confederation of Indians. They also stood with Andrew Jackson at the Battle of New Orleans, where Britain's plans to occupy the Mississippi River Valley were defeated. After the War of 1812, the Choctaws signed a treaty with the United States in 1816 at Fort St. Stephens to clear any Choctaw claims to Creek lands already ceded. Though the Choctaws received much praise for their bravery, sacrifice, and loyalty to the American cause, the Americans continued to erode Choctaw culture with increased importation of white religions and commercial practices. Missionaries and merchants formed a vanguard for restless white settlers and frontiersmen who did not take kindly to borders, especially those of Indian country. They asked what right Indians had to stand in their way—the way of progress. Racism fed many of their beliefs. They rationalized. Their religions permitted them to see themselves as being correct and superior in almost all of their actions. At first the American government tried to put restraints and controls on the frontiersmen, but the frontiersmen picked and chose the laws they would obey. With this mindset, the white community in Mississippi gained statehood in 1817.

White Mississippians did not want another sovereign nation within the state's borders, and they declared Choctaws must be citizens of the state—not of the Indian nation. State officials fussed and fretted at protective federal regulations concerning the Indians. Reasonable people, the Choctaws tried to protect and preserve their family livelihoods legally. Clearly most Choctaws preferred a low-key, individualistic, farming-hunting lifestyle enhanced with an almost universal love of ballgames. Their customs of hospitality let them

Choctaw ballgame by George Catlin. Courtesy of Mississippi Department of
Archives and History.

easily accept outsiders into their communities. By the time their country fell
within United States dominion, the nation had a large population of mixed-
bloods who served as a cultural bridge between the white and Indian worlds.
No one could have logically considered the Choctaws a hostile people, but
fresh memories of the Creek War caused many white Mississippians concern
about Indians in general.

In the Treaty of Doaks' Stand in 1820, the Choctaws ceded 13,000,000 acres
of land in Mississippi and Alabama to the United States in return for land in
Arkansas, west of the Mississippi. The land remaining within the Choctaw
nation east of the river was to remain Indian country until such time as "said
nation shall become so civilized and enlightened as to be made citizens of the
United States. . . ." Indians wishing to relocate to the land west of the Mississippi were to be given a blanket, a kettle, a rifle, bullet molds, and a year's
worth of ammunition and corn. With hunting and these provisions, immigrants should be able to establish themselves in the new territory. For Choc-

taws remaining east of the Mississippi, the treaty provided for schools, an Indian police corps called the Light Horse, the seizing of illegal whiskey, and individual pensions and payments. Andrew Jackson and Thomas Hinds negotiated the treaty for the United States. The three division chiefs signing the treaty were Puckshenubbee, Pushmataha, and Mushulatubbee. But the Arkansas land ceded to the Choctaws had already been settled by white men and the treaty had to be renegotiated with the three chiefs at Washington, D. C., in 1825. Puckshenubee died on the journey to the American capitol, and shortly after arriving there, Pushmataha became ill, died, and was buried in the city. Only Mushulatubbee was left to sign the new treaty with Secretary of War John C. Calhoun.

While in Washington, the Choctaw delegation heard talk of plans for a removal treaty that would dissolve the Choctaw nation east of the Mississippi. In an address before Congress they asked for compassion for the evolving Choctaw culture and for brotherhood. If their words reached back to Mississippi, they had no positive effect on white sentiment. By this time the Choctaws had a working government with a constitution, a police force, and a court system. Shortly after the 1825 treaty, the Mississippi legislature passed laws declaring the Choctaw tribal government invalid and tribal laws null and void. Unless appointed by and operating on behalf of the state, Choctaw officials were declared outlaws.

At this point the United States federal government had an opportunity to honor agreements with the Choctaws and curb the aggressive stance of the state legislature. Instead, the southern-dominated federal Congress chose to pass the Indian Removal Act in 1830 which eventually impacted on all the Indian nations in the Southeast. The Choctaws came to grips with the future the Americans planned for them when they signed the Treaty of Dancing Rabbit Creek in September 1830. The Treaty of Dancing Rabbit Creek declared all other agreements with the Choctaws "null and void." Removal of the majority of the 20,000 to 25,000 member tribe was to be completed by 1833. The three principal chiefs negotiating the treaty of Dancing Rabbit Creek were Greenwood Laflore (Leflore), Mushulatubbe, and Nutackachie. The United States gained 10,423,130 acres in Mississippi and Alabama from the treaty.

The treaty offered individual tribesmen a choice of giving up their Choctaw identity and remaining in Mississippi as citizens of the state on their own plots of land, or of removing to Oklahoma where they could pursue their traditional

Above, left: Pushmataha. Photograph courtesy of Robert E. Hauberg, Jr. *Above, right:* Choctaw Chief Mushu-latubbe. Courtesy of Mississippi Department of Archives and History. *Left:* Greenwood Le Flore. Courtesy of Mississippi Department of Archives and History.

Granite Boulder marking the site of Dancing Rabbit Creek Treaty of 1830.
Photograph courtesy of Jeffrey Robbins.

way of life. Many who wanted to stay in Mississippi and agreed to the terms
were denied the opportunity by the Indian agent William Ward, a notorious
alcoholic, who officials later claimed must have been drunk when processing
applications of those who wished to stay—because the applications were never
recorded. Apparently Ward's intent was to "remove" as many Indians as possible. His efforts were later officially censured by a government which had to
endure claims hearings and adverse publicity for well over a century.

Among the Choctaws who did stay in Mississippi were mixed-bloods who were accepted as white and an estimated several thousand traditional Choctaws. These traditional Choctaws would be subjected to another "removal" at the end of the century. The betrayal of trust and the sacrifice of one people's liberty for the benefit of another are constantly recurring themes in the saga of the United States' relations with the Choctaws, while the government treaties tell a story of political intrigue and a continuing clash over state and federal rights.

Notes

1. The author wishes to acknowledge that a portion of this manuscript was researched and written by Mary Ann Wells, who has recently finished an extensive project with the Mississippi Department of Archives and History to produce a readable, popular history of the region comprising the present state of Mississippi from the time of European contact until the United States gained control of the area following the 1795 Treaty of San Lorenzo Real.

2. The spelling of Choctaw and other Indian names varies tremendously, depending on the scribe, and spellings are not necessarily consistent even within a single document. Names are printed as they appear in the various documents, with the exceptions of standard spellings of ones generally familiar (such as Pushmataha).

Suggested Readings

Carter, Clarence E. *Territorial Papers of the United States.* 26 vols. *The Territory of Mississippi*, vols. 5 and 6. Washington: Government Printing Office, 1937–1938.

Cotterill, Robert S. *The Southern Indians: The Story of the Five Civilized Tribes Before Removal.* Civilization of the American Indian Series, 38. Norman: University of Oklahoma Press, 1954.

Cushman, Horatio B., *History of the Choctaw, Chickasaw and Natchez Indians.* Ed. and intro. Angie Debo. Stillwater, Oklahoma: Redlands Press, 1962.

DeRosier, Arthur, Jr. *The Removal of the Choctaw Indians.* Knoxville: University of Tennessee Press, 1972.

Haynes, Robert V. *The Natchez District and the American Revolution.* Jackson: University Press of Mississippi, 1976.

Holmes, Jack D. L. *Gayoso.* Baton Rouge: Louisiana State University Press, 1965.

Kappler, Charles, ed. and comp. *Indian Affairs: Laws and Treaties.* 4 vols. Washington: Government Printing Office, 1904–1929.

Kidwell, Clara Sue, and Charles Roberts. *The Choctaws: A Critical Bibliography*. Bloomington: Indiana University Press, 1980.

Kinnaird, Lawrence, ed. *Annual Report of the American Historical Association for the Year 1945*. 4 vols. Washington: Government Printing Office, 1946.

Peters, Richard, ed. *United States Statutes at Large, vol. 7, Treaties Between the United States and the Indian Tribes*. Boston: Charles C. Little and James Brown, 1848.

Prucha, Francis Paul. *A Bibliographical Guide to the History of Indian-White Relations in the United States*. Chicago: University of Chicago Press, 1977.

Royce, Charles C. *Indian Land Cessions in the United States*. Washington: Government Printing Office, 1900 (reprint, 1971).

Rowland, Dunbar, ed. *Mississippi Provincial Archives, English Dominion, 1763–1766*. Nashville: Press of Brandon, 1911.

Wells, Mary Ann. *Native Land: Mississippi 1540–1798*. Forthcoming.

Wells, Samuel J. "Choctaw Mixed Bloods and the Advent of Removal." Ph.D. Dissertation, University of Southern Mississippi, 1987.

Wells, Samuel J. "Rum, Skins, and Powder: A Choctaw Interpreter and the Treaty of Mount Dexter," *Chronicles of Oklahoma* (1982–83), 4:422–428.

Wells, Samuel J. "International Causes of the Treaty of Mount Dexter," *Journal of Mississippi History* (August 1986) 48:177–185.

Wells, Samuel J. "Treaties and the Choctaw People," in *Tribal Government: A New Era*, ed. William Brescia. Philadelphia, Mississippi: Choctaw Heritage Press, 1982, 14–18.

The Mississippi Choctaws
in the Nineteenth Century

Clara Sue Kidwell

The Choctaws in the early nineteenth century lived in the central part of Mississippi. Their villages lay primarily on the ridges that divided the watersheds of the Big Black, the Pearl, and the Tombigbee Rivers. Their government was loosely vested in the three district chiefs, Puckshanubbee in the Western District, Mushulatubbee in the Northeast, and Pushmataha in the Southern district. These territories reflected earlier political divisions within the tribe.

Although the men had originally hunted to the Tombigbee on the east and beyond the Mississippi on the west, the life styles of the Choctaws were changing in the early nineteenth century. They maintained traditional beliefs in the spirits of the natural world. They revered Nanih Waiya, the sacred mound, as the site of their origin as a people. Men went into the woods to find personal spirit helpers. Communities still competed with each other in ball games. Traditional funeral practices were changing, however. Bodies were no longer exposed on platforms to decay before the power of the sun but were buried. The mourning rituals now included setting poles over the grave and ritual crying (hence the name "cries" for traditional funerals).

With the westward expansion of the United States, white settlers moved into the Choctaw territory and married Choctaw women. Hardy Perry and Louis Durant introduced livestock in the 1790s, and Choctaw families began to use cattle and pigs (which foraged semi-wild in the woods) for food. By the early nineteenth century, Choctaw settlements were shifting into the northeastern part of the nation where the rich prairie land supported cattle grazing. Cattle began to replace deer as food largely because the deerskin trade led to the decline of the deer population in the traditional hunting areas.

As the deer disappeared from their territories, the Choctaws began to cede the less productive hunting lands. Beginning in 1801, they made a series of treaties with the United States government that gradually whittled away at their boundaries—at Fort Adams in 1801, Fort Confederation in 1802, Hoe Buckintoopa in 1803, Mount Dexter in 1805, the Choctaw Trading House at St. Stephens in 1816, and at Doaks' Stand in 1820. The Choctaws traded land for what they hoped would be settled boundaries and, in 1816, for annuities. As many realized that the old life of hunting and moving freely was now constrained, the leaders Puckshanubbee and Pushmataha wrote to the President of the United States asking for schools and missionaries. In 1818, Cyrus Kingsbury and Loring Williams, missionaries of the American Board of Commissioners for Foreign Missions, established their first station at Elliot. Support for the mission came in part from the Choctaw annuities. In 1820 the missionaries opened a second station at Mayhew.

Mississippi statehood in 1817 brought a new wave of white settlers into the state and created greater pressure for the Choctaws to give up their lands. George Poindexter proposed in Congress that the Choctaws not be allowed to hunt west of the Mississippi. Although this may seem contrary to a desire for them to leave the state and move west, it was actually a ploy to force them to cede lands in Mississippi in exchange for a guaranteed right to their traditional territory in the west. The federal government pursued a strategy to separate "savage" Indians, who still lived by hunting, from "civilized" ones who were willing to lead the lives of settled farmers. At treaty negotiations in 1820, Andrew Jackson threatened the Choctaws with the loss of all rights to their lands west of the Mississippi if they did not sign. The strategy worked. The Treaty of Doaks' Stand in 1820 marked the first large cession of the Choctaw homeland. In exchange for a guarantee of their right to live and hunt west of the Mississippi, the Choctaws gave up approximately thirteen million acres of

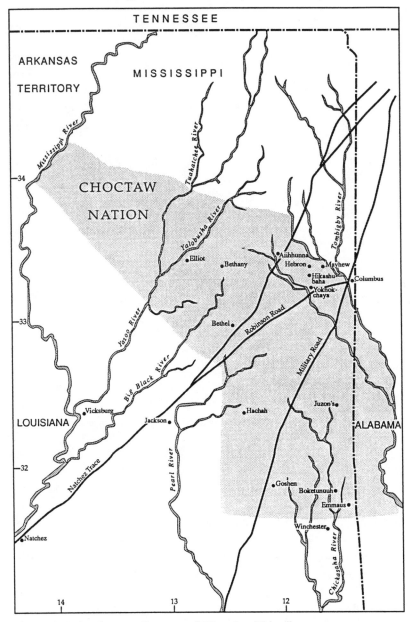

Choctaw Nation in 1820. Courtesy of Clara Sue Kidwell.

land in western Mississippi for about twenty million acres in Arkansas and Oklahoma.

Among the provisions of the 1820 treaty was one calling for the sale of fifty-four sections of land to raise a fund for schools. The Choctaw leaders were eager to have their children educated in the white man's ways so that they could better deal with their white neighbors. They were also eager to have blacksmith shops to deal with the new mechanical devices that were rapidly becoming part of their culture. The missionaries of the American Board expanded their school system into the Southern district with the money from the treaty.

Despite the guarantee of the western land, however, the boundary of the Arkansas territory had to be adjusted because white settlers had moved onto Choctaw lands. Outraged statements from Arkansas representatives and newspapers led the government to pressure the Choctaws to cede those lands rather than try to move the settlers.

The three district chiefs, Puckshanubbee, Pushmataha, and Mushulatubbee, set out for Washington, D.C. in the fall of 1824 to negotiate the treaty. But Puckshanubbee died in a rather mysterious accident on the journey, and Pushmataha was found dead in his hotel room in Washington, the victim of an unknown ailment. The treaty was finally negotiated by Mushulatubbee and other members of the Choctaw delegation—Robert Cole, who was Puckshanubbee's spokesman, and Nitakuche, who later succeeded Pushmataha.

The passing of two strong full-blood leaders precipitated a political crisis within the tribe that reflected the changes that were going on in the lives of the Choctaws. One of the new leaders of the tribe was David Folsom, son of a Choctaw mother and a Scotch-Irish father. He had grown up at Pigeon Roost, his father's trading post on the Natchez Trace. He was also a strong supporter of the American Board missions. That support brought him into conflict with Mushulatubbee, the remaining traditional chief. Folsom wanted an expanded network of schools in Mississippi. Mushulatubbee pledged the whole education annuity from the treaty to the establishment of a school in Kentucky, the Choctaw Academy. He claimed that the Choctaw children in the mission schools had not been well educated. The missionaries found themselves caught in a political struggle between Mushulatubbee as the remaining representative of the traditional full-blood leadership of the tribe and the new mixed-blood leaders who supported the schools.

The Choctaws were fighting to survive in the state by demonstrating their ability to adapt to the white man's ways. In 1826 they adopted a constitution that established a centralized, representative form of government. But they were also fighting among themselves. The signers of the constitution were Tapanahuma for the southern district, David Folsom for the Northeast, and Greenwood Leflore for the western district. But Mushulatubbee and Nitaku-che still considered themselves chiefs of the northeast and southern districts, and Tapanahuma and Leflore had been elected by factions. Finally, at a council in 1829, Greenwood Leflore was elected sole chief of the Choctaw nation, an act bitterly opposed by Mushulatubbee and Nitakuche.

The political turmoil was complicated by the threat of a forced removal. Although the Choctaws had supported schools and churches and adopted a constitution, they were still considered a backward and savage people by many citizens of the state, and white settlers looked longingly at their lands. For Mushulatubbee, and for the many Choctaws who still lived by hunting, the move to the west was a reasonable prospect, although the lands there were dry and open, rather than the well-watered and wooded lands that they were used to. The new leaders, mixed-bloods, were well established on the land—as traders, slaveholders, and planters. They were committed to fight for the Choctaw homeland in ways that Mushulatubbee was not. While the Choctaw leaders had always realized that their lives were changing and that they must accommodate to new ways, Mushulatubbee had chosen the traditional way of hunting and removal, while Leflore and Folsom had chosen the way of educa-tion and Christianity in order to stay in the state.

The clash of cultures led almost to civil war in 1830, as Mushulatubbee and Nitakuche faced off against Leflore and Folsom at a council. Although a handshake between Folsom and Nitakuche reaffirmed the unity of the tribe, it could not avert the pressure of the United States government on the Choctaws to cede their lands and move west.

The major incentive was the threat of losing Choctaw autonomy to the state of Mississippi. The threat had been presented in the negotiations leading to the 1820 treaty. It became real when the state extended its jurisdiction over the Choctaw lands and people in January of 1830 and forbade anyone to act as a Choctaw chief. Faced with this reality, the Choctaws entered on negotiations for a removal treaty with John Eaton and John Coffee in September of 1830.

The majority of tribal members who assembled at the treaty ground rejected outright the idea of giving up their homeland and left after they thought the negotiations were complete. A small group of chiefs and headmen remained,

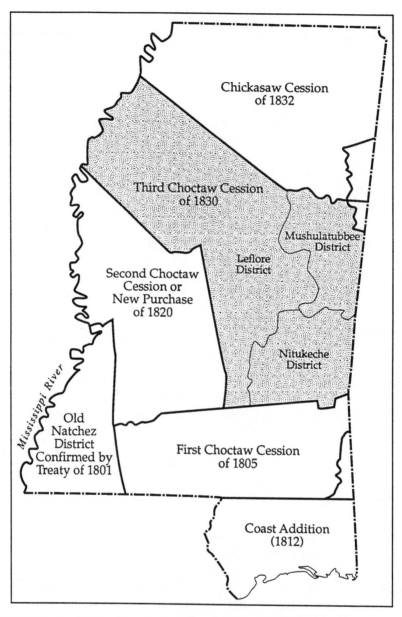

Indian Cessions during the early nineteenth century. The Choctaw treaty of 1830 required the Indians to move to Oklahoma. Courtesy of Clara Sue Kidwell.

however, and on September 27, 1830, 171 Choctaws, including Leflore, Mush-ulatubbee, Nitakuche, David Folsom, and Robert Cole, signed the treaty.

The Choctaw leaders had learned well about the value of land. They agreed to move, but they laid on the government significant provisions concerning the land that they had ceded. If they could not remain in Mississippi as a tribe, those individuals who wanted to stay could take claims under the fourteenth article of the treaty for themselves and their children. Greenwood Leflore had negotiated this provision specifically with Eaton and Coffee as a way of getting the treaty approved. In the nineteenth article, the Choctaws who moved west were to be compensated for the loss of their farms. In other articles, individuals who had served the nation were to receive land. These provisions of the treaty threw a significant cloud over title to the newly ceded lands.

Approximately fifteen thousand Choctaws moved west of the Mississippi after 1830. Another five thousand or so stayed behind in Mississippi, now as individual citizens. They had no special legal rights. Many attempted to take individual claims under the fourteenth article of the treaty. The treaty required them to register with William Ward, the Choctaw agent, within six months of the ratification of the treaty (February 26, 1830), and they must then live on the land for five years thereafter in order to secure title. However, Ward did not receive his instructions until May of 1831, and he submitted two different registers of the claimants (one contained 68 names, the other 71 names). Since his register was to be the final determinant of who was to receive land, the variations were troublesome.

Choctaw land was now on the open market, and the federal government moved quickly to open the Choctaw cession at public sales, which began in 1833. The land was surveyed and laid out in sections for sale. Land fueled the flush times of Mississippi. Those who controlled large blocks of land could profit at the expense of settlers who wanted cheap land.

While the government prepared for public sales of the Choctaw lands in 1833, George Martin was appointed to mark individual Choctaw land claims to exclude them from sale. But Martin couldn't get the vital survey maps he needed because the public land offices were using their copies for the public sales. As he traveled through the Choctaw country, Martin heard numerous complaints that Ward had refused to register Choctaw claims. Although he suspected that land speculators were prompting Choctaws to file false claims, he dutifully reported the complaints to the federal government. Because of his report, the U.S. Congress appointed a commission in 1837 to investigate the claims. Although the first commission's charge expired in 1838, the volume of claims was so great that Congress revived the commission in 1842, and its hearings dragged on through 1845. It proved indeed that a number of white men who represented Choctaw claims had signed contracts with their clients to put forth claims in exchange for part of the land that might be awarded. It also proved that many Choctaws who had remained on their land were driven off by white men who had bought the land at public sales before Martin had marked their claims.

As their lands disappeared into the hands of white men, many moved to settle near a few Choctaws who had managed to secure title and owned their homes. Jim Shoate's and Samuel Cobb's lands became centers of Choctaw groups. Others remained on traditional lands near the "Yellow Butcher" (Lobutcha) Creek or moved to areas such as Sinesha and Beasha Creeks.

To clear land titles in Mississippi, the U.S. Congress voted in 1842 to grant land scrip to Choctaws who could prove valid claims to land that had already been sold at public sales. In 1852, Congress provided money in place of scrip for Choctaw claims. Only 164 of 1099 claims investigated by the two commissions were satisfied with patents rather than scrip, and many of those went to white assignees of the claimants.

By 1853, the Choctaws were largely people without rights to land, although some still lived where they always had. They had no recognition as an Indian tribe. A census of the Choctaws taken in 1853 showed a population of 2068 in Mississippi, Alabama, and Louisiana. They still identified themselves by traditional clan or extended family groups. The Six Towns lived in Jasper and Newton Counties, although many had left the state and lived in St. Tammany Parish in Louisiana. The Chunkees lived in Newton, Jasper, and Lauderdale Counties. The Moglushas lived in Newton and Neshoba Counties. The Yoknuknes lived in Carroll and Leake Counties. The Pearl Rivers and Haloonlowahs lived in Neshoba County near the Pearl. The Bogue Chittos lived in the Northeast part of Neshoba County, and the Tallachulaks lived in southeastern Kemper County.

The Choctaws were an anomaly in Mississippi—neither white nor black, free, but not landholders. They spoke a different language, and they held to their own customs and communities. During the Civil War, some 200 of them fought as the First Choctaw Battalion, although they were recruited not by the state but by Arnold Spann for the Confederate government. A number were captured in a battle at Ponchatoula in Louisiana, and thirteen died in a Union

Jack Amos, grandnephew of Pushmataha. Amos led a group of Choctaws who rescued Confederate soldiers from a train wreck at the Chunky River, near Newton, Mississippi, in February 1863. Photograph from *Paths to the Past, an Overview History of Lauderdale County, Mississippi* by Laura Nan Fairley and James T. Dawson. Courtesy of Annie Rose Mabry.

prison in Port Hamilton, New York. In Mississippi, a number of Choctaw men rescued survivors when a train carrying Confederate troops plunged off a bridge over the Chunky River in Newton County.

After the war, the Choctaws became largely invisible in Mississippi society. As the South struggled with Reconstruction, the Choctaws lived quietly as sharecroppers and wage laborers. The Bay Indians, some 200 people, lived in Hancock County. They had moved en masse from the Leaf River area under the threat of being dispossessed by white men and had settled near a promi- nent Roman Catholic landholder whose daughter had established a school for them. The Tallachuluk band lived in southwestern Kemper County. Other groups were around Union and Stratton, and the Bogue Chittos constituted a large group in northeastern Neshoba County.

Choctaw women made baskets and gathered firewood and traveled on foot to New Orleans and Mobile to sell them in the public markets. A significant amount of subsistence hunting probably still went on. Their children were largely unschooled. Poor and picturesque, they survived as a distinctive group.

The Choctaws were both excluded from Mississippi society, and kept their distance from it. Their language was an important marker of their identity, and they gathered for ballgames and funerals. They were largely ignored by Mis- sissippians, but they were noticed by others. In 1881 Francis Janssens, a Belgian priest who was bishop of the Catholic diocese at Natchez, observed their poverty during a trip through central Mississippi. Through his efforts, a Catholic mission was established at Tucker in 1883. The Baptist church had maintained some missionary efforts among the Choctaws who remained after removal and in 1881 sent a call to the Choctaw/Chickasaw Baptist Association in Oklahoma for a missionary. An Oklahoma Choctaw Baptist minister, Peter Folsom, arrived in 1882 and established three congregations. Although he died less than a year after his arrival, his successors, including at least three native Choctaw preachers, carried on his work and established a network of Choctaw Baptist churches. In 1892, William Carmack established a Methodist mission near the Tallachuluk Indians.

An important part of the missionary spirit was to buy land so that the converts could be brought together around the church. The Catholic Church acquired some four thousand acres around Tucker. The Methodist missionary Carmack bought 160 acres. Finally, from being a landless people, some Choc- taws actually became land holders, if not land owners.

In 1888 the state also appropriated funds for Indian schools which had been

Holy Rosary Indian Church in the Tucker Community (approximately 10 miles south of Philadelphia, Mississippi). Courtesy of Archives, Catholic Diocese of Jackson, Mississippi.

started by the Catholic mission. These schools were part of the state's public education system until 1900. At the Catholic school at Tucker, Henry S. Halbert was the first teacher. He had lived among the Choctaws and become fluent in their language, and he taught reading and writing in Choctaw to his pupils. The texts and orthography that he used were those first produced by the Presbyterian missionaries who had worked among the Choctaws after 1818. Although the earlier missionaries had intended to assimilate the Choctaws into American society, their efforts contributed to the later preservation of Choctaw language that helped the Mississippi Choctaws to retain their identity.

Missionaries trained native ministers who preached in Choctaw. Churches provided a focus for Choctaw community life and culture. They could hear sermons in their own language (and oratory was one of the skills valued in

Choctaw man (Will E. Morris) beating drum for dance and ball-play. Photograph by M. R. Harrington, 1908. Photograph courtesy of Museum of the American Indian, Heye Foundation.

Choctaw congregation at Tucker, Mississippi. Photograph courtesy of University Libraries of Marquette University and Archives, Catholic Diocese of Jackson, Mississippi.

traditional Choctaw communities). They could sing, and they had always been noted by other tribes as singers. They could hold feasts and ball games on the church grounds. Although Christian denominations may have intended to assimilate the Choctaws to Christian values and American culture, churches were places where the Choctaws could come together to sing and speak Choctaw and be recognized as a group.

By the end of the nineteenth century, the Choctaws, although not recognized by the state, still maintained distinctive communities. But the threat of removal appeared once again, as it had in the first half of the century. The Curtis Act in 1889 provided for the allotment of lands in the Indian Territory (Oklahoma), and the Mississippi Choctaws were given the opportunity to take claims in Oklahoma and move west. The basic question was whether the Mississippi Choctaws were still members of the Choctaw nation now in

Oklahoma. Had they given up their tribal rights entirely, or could they still claim tribal membership by moving to Oklahoma to live on and claim land there?

The Curtis Act caused a legal reexamination of the status of the Choctaws in Mississippi. One result was that the state suspended its funding for Indian schools, and the schools disappear from the annual school reports for the state. The Act would ultimately lead to a second removal and disruption of Choctaw communities.

At the end of the nineteenth century, Choctaws in Mississippi had found their own places in the culture and society of the state. They had a sense of their community, their language, and their customs. They had found outsiders who created for them the structures recognizable to the larger society— churches and schools. Those structures would ultimately allow them to be recognized as a distinctive group in Mississippi society with the establishment of their reservation in 1918.

Sources

American Board of Commissioners for Foreign Missions, Papers, Series 18.3.4., Houghton Library, Harvard University.

American State Papers: Documents, Legislative and Executive of the Congress of the United States (38 vols.; Washington: Gales and Seaton, 1832–61); Series 2, Indian Affairs, 2 vols.

Choctaw vs. U.S., U.S. Court of Claims case 12742.

Debo, Angie. *The Rise and Fall of the Choctaw Republic*. Norman: University of Oklahoma Press, 1934.

DeRosier, Arthur H., Jr. *The Removal of the Choctaw Indians*. New York: Harper & Row Publishers, 1972.

Halbert, H. S., "District Divisions of the Choctaw Nation," *Publications of the Alabama Historical Society, Miscellaneous Collection*, vol. 1, (1901), 375–85.

Kappler, Charles J., *Indian Affairs: Laws and Treaties*. 5 vols. Washington, D.C.: Government Printing Office, 1904, 1941.

National Archives, Record Group 75, Choctaw Removal Records, National Archives, Record Group 75, Choctaw Removal Records, entries 260, 262, 268, 269, 271, 272, 274, 275, 277, 278, 280.

White, Richard. *Roots of Dependency*. Lincoln: University of Nebraska Press, 1983.

PART TWO

ENCOUNTERS
Native Americans, Europeans, Africans

Introduction

Charles D. Lowery

It is now well established fact that Christopher Columbus's epochal 1492 voyage occurred some five hundred years after Europeans first discovered what came to be called the New World. During the course of the ninth and tenth centuries the Norsemen, aided by a string of stepping-stone islands linking Europe and America, crossed from their Scandinavian homeland and planted colonies in Iceland and Greenland. Sometime around the year 1000 A.D., the Viking captain Leif Ericson, driven before a storm, missed Greenland and made land on the North American coast, in a country where wild grapes grew and which, appropriately enough, he named Vinland. Norse adventurers subsequently colonized this country, which archeological evidence indicates was located at L'Anse aux Meadows, Newfoundland. But this settlement lasted only a few years. The Viking encounter with and occupation of North America was superficial and ephemeral. What is most remarkable about the Vikings, says historian Daniel Boorstin in his book *The Discoverers*, is not that they actually reached America, but that "they reached America and even settled for a while, without *discovering* America."[1] Because Europe was not ready for expansion in the eleventh century, she did not follow up the Norse discovery. Vinland was soon forgotten.

During the next five hundred years, political, social, and economic developments transformed Europe. In the following essay entitled "The European Background in the Late Fifteenth Century," Paul Hoffman shows how these changes created dynamic and expansive nation states eager after Columbus's voyages to capitalize on opportunities the New World afforded to enlarge their power and national boundaries and increase their wealth. From the Old World the colonizers transported such fundamental things as economic habits, religious faiths, social values, and governmental forms, which were modified and transformed by the New World.

In some ways Mississippi before 1699 was like Vinland. It was known by a few adventurous Europeans to be a bountiful, well watered, and fertile land eminently suited for agricultural settlement. But as Robert Weddle shows in his survey, "European Interest in the Gulf Coast, 1500–1699," for more than two hundred years following Columbus the Mississippi country attracted only the passing interest of European colonial powers. Before 1699 no more than a handful of Spanish and French adventurers explored or touched on Mississippi, and none attempted to colonize it. Its remoteness from the sea lanes and trade routes, together with its apparent lack of natural resources capable of producing quick or easy wealth, made it unattractive to European adventurers, entrepreneurs, and colonizers. They concentrated their efforts elsewhere.

At the end of the seventeenth century the situation changed. The European colonial powers finally took note of Mississippi. France led the way. From their New France strongholds at Quebec and Montreal, Frenchmen such as Father Jacques Marquette, Louis Joliet, and Robert Cavelier de La Salle explored the Great Lakes and the Mississippi Valley. When La Salle descended the great river to its mouth in 1682, New France's expansionist design became apparent to her New World rivals. By building a chain of outposts stretching from the St. Lawrence to the Great Lakes and down the Mississippi to the Gulf coast, France would gain control of the North American heartland. British colonies along the Atlantic coast, hemmed in by the French in the Mississippi Valley and by the Spanish in Florida, would be encircled.

Spanish hegemony in Florida and the Gulf coast region, unchallenged since the sixteenth century, was imperiled by the French incursions. When La Salle established a colony at Matagorda Bay on the Texas coast following his descent of the Mississippi, Spain countered by planting a colony at Pensacola in 1698. The following year Pierre le Moyne d'Iberville built Ft. Maurepas at Biloxi and founded Mobile three years later. By the time they established New Orleans in

1718, the French had driven a large wedge between Spanish colonies in Florida and Mexico. The stage was set for the great contest for empire between France, Spain, and England.

That rivalry, as it affected Mississippi, is detailed by William Cash in his essay on "The European Colonization of Mississippi." He shows how the French-Spanish confrontation in this borderland region was ended by the Seven Years' War, only to be replaced by a new rivalry between Spain and England for control of the country. This contest was fueled by the territorial arrangements resulting from the Treaty of Paris ending the war in 1763. France was removed from North America altogether. She transferred to Spain New Orleans and her vast Louisiana territory, bounded on the south by the Gulf of Mexico, on the east by the Mississippi River, and extending northward into the interior an indefinite distance. England came into possession of both East and West Florida. Instead of a divided Spanish empire penetrated by a French wedge on the lower Mississippi, there emerged from the Great War for Empire a solid Spanish territory to the west of the Mississippi and a solid English territory to the east. The English and Anglo-Americans, and after 1783 the Americans, were left to contest the Mississippi country with the Spanish.

When the British came in 1763 to take possession of the former Spanish colony, they described the Mississippi country as a sandy, barren, fever-ridden wasteland hardly fit for human habitation. The few Europeans who inhabited the country were described as impoverished "riffraff" who managed to eke out a meager existence raising cattle and producing naval stores.[2] The old French settlement at Biloxi had only a few survivors, and the French settlements along the Mississippi between the Walnut Hills and Baton Rouge, which had seemed so promising in the early 1700s, had not recovered from the effects of the war with the Natchez Indians three decades earlier. Except for Native Americans, Mississippi was virtually devoid of population. If their new colony was to grow and prosper, the British would have to find ways to attract settlers to farm and people the land.

Despite a liberal land policy and other enticements held out to prospective emigrants, the British authorities initially were unsuccessful in attracting new settlers. They induced a few Swiss and German inhabitants of Louisiana living along the lower Mississippi to cross over into British territory. But most of Spain's Louisiana subjects, believing that the lands along the Mississippi Gulf coast were infertile, chose to remain on the rich Mississippi delta of the Isle of Orleans, in Spanish territory. A small contingent of French Huguenots, brought over by the province's lieutenant governor, Montfort Browne, settled in 1766 at Dauphin Island near Mobile, but they did not remain. Only a trickle of British families came into the province in the early years, and most of this migration went to the Pensacola area. Interest in Mississippi was not really kindled until after 1668, when Lieutenant Governor Browne conducted an exploration and inspection tour of the western part of the province, which carried him to the Natchez area.

Browne was enthralled by what he found. He informed the home government that the soil all along the Mississippi was exceptionally fertile. The Natchez area was so rich and beautiful that he would happily spend the balance of his life there. To Lord Hillsborough he rhapsodically wrote that everywhere he discovered the "most charming prospects in the world, extensive plains intermixed with beautiful hills, and small rivers; here are, my lord, fruit trees of most excellent kinds, the grape, peach, plum, apricot, apple, pear, figs, mulberry, cherry, persimmon, medlars, and strawberries as good in their kind as any in the world and in as great abundance."[3]

As Browne made plans to take advantage of his happy discovery, other explorations followed. In 1770 another provincial official, Elias Durnford, confirmed Browne's findings. Not only were the lands along the Mississippi River, and particularly in the Natchez country, "superior in goodness to what I have ever imagined," but so also were the lands along the colony's southern border.[4] In the same year an official who had lived for many years in the Pensacola area, Edward Mease, conducted his own tour of the Natchez country. In a long narrative report to Lord Hillsborough, he ecstatically wrote that "no lands in North America can possibly exceed the banks of this noble river in fertility." From its bluffs one enjoyed "as noble and extensive a prospect as can gratify the eye. . . . Looking eastward [from Natchez] you see . . . a fine undulating country which even the celebrated Campania of Rome cannot exceed in beauty."[5]

These exploratory forays constituted the real "discovery" of Mississippi, which for 250 years had been largely ignored except to serve as a pawn in the European contest for colonial empire. Unlike the French and Spanish before them, the British were in a position administratively and economically to take advantage of their discovery. Eager to plant the fertile alluvial soil of the Mississippi delta, which they believed would produce abundant crops of indigo, tobacco, cotton, and grains, they quickly took the first steps to populate and develop the country. Those same British provincial officials who first explored the western region—Browne, Durnford, Mease, and others—staked out the first claims to princely tracts of land. British emigrants began to find their way to Britain's westernmost province. More important, this first trickle of settlers opened the way to a major movement of people south and west from the backcountry of the original thirteen English colonies.

These Anglo-American denizens of the backcountry, following the easiest avenues of travel, the interior rivers, moved first along the Holston and Cumberland and Tennessee rivers to the Alabama and Tombigbee rivers. Descending those streams to their convergence with the Tensas above Mobile Bay, they established thriving communities in the central sector of the Mississippi territory. But the flow of settlement soon turned westward and southward to the Mississippi delta, converging on the Natchez country. By 1770 the trickle had turned into a steady flow. From western New York and Pennsylvania by way of the Ohio and Mississippi; from Virginia and Maryland via the Holston and Tennessee; from the Carolinas and Georgia through the gaps and passes of the Appalachians; from Connecticut by ship through the Gulf of Mexico and thence by boat up the Mississippi, they came by boat and barge, by cart and wagon, on horseback and on foot, to settle the new land. Most were small movements—single families, combined family groups, and parties of individuals who banded together for protection.

Occasionally, larger group movements occurred, as in the case of the company of New England families that settled along the Mississippi in the Natchez district in the early 1770s. These farming families came primarily from the lower Connecticut River valley. The heads of the families were veterans of the Seven Years' War who were rewarded for their military service with land bounties in Mississippi. In the spring of 1773 the Connecticut Company of Military Adventurers sent a reconnoitering party to explore the tract of 380,000 prime acres lying along a ten-mile stretch of the Mississippi that had been reserved for them. Israel Putnam, the party leader, was profoundly impressed by the fertility of the delta lands, which he believed were equal to if not "superior to any in North America." It was "a very easy country to live in," he said, where "independent fortunes may be made . . . equal to almost any in the world."[6] Within a few short months the largest single pre-Revolutionary incident of migration from the eastern colonies to Mississippi began. By the outbreak of the Revolution, which put an end to the movement, at least four hundred New England families, and perhaps more, had moved to their new home in Mississippi.

During the decade of peace preceding the American Revolution, the British colony of West Florida, and especially that portion which in 1798 became the Mississippi Territory, was transformed from a sleepy, unpopulated, backwater province to a much publicized boom country whose fertile soil and mild climate made it, in the opinion of its promoters and colonizers, a new Promised Land. Mississippi's first boom period witnessed a rapid growth in population and the swift spread of settlement. From the Spanish-French borderland, from East Florida, from Britain's eastern colonies, and from the mother country itself, colonists flocked to the new country. More than two hundred miles of land fronting the Mississippi River was opened up, and land grants along the Gulf coast and Mobile Bay increased sharply. By 1774 the population of the colony, according to one official estimate, was just under 5,000, of which approximately one-fourth were slaves. More than 3,000 of these people were clustered along the eastern bank of the Mississippi from the Yazoo River south to the Iberville River. The province was still thinly peopled, with a population density, excluding Native Americans, of only one settler for every eleven square miles. But a decade earlier there had been practically no white population in the province. During the Revolution, when the province served as an asylum for refugee Loyalists, its population would continue to grow.

At the Treaty of Paris, 1783, Britain ceded her West Florida colony to Spain. The northern boundary of the province was unspecified. In preliminary articles with the United States signed in 1782, Britain granted to her former colonies all her western lands lying between the Appalachians and the Mississippi River, bounded on the north by the Great Lakes and Canada and on the south by the thirty-first parallel of latitude. When Spain took possession of West Florida after 1783, she claimed as the province's northern boundary the line of 32°28′. The disputed Yazoo strip, bounded on the east by the Chattahoochee River and on the west by the Mississippi, embraced all the land between 31° and 32°28′. Included in this valuable parcel of disputed real estate was the Natchez district, where most of the province's white population was concentrated. Spain and the United States would not settle the dispute until 1795, when the Treaty of San Lorenzo established the thirty-first parallel as the northern boundary of West Florida.

During the years the Yazoo strip was disputed by the two countries, Spain attempted to win over the Natchez inhabitants by enacting a liberal land policy that enabled the settlers to increase their holdings. This, coupled with a lenient governing hand and special government subsidies for producing such agricultural products as tobacco, kept the settlers acquiescent. A few American emigrants continued to come into the country despite the Spanish presence, though the heavy flow of the pre-Revolutionary decade stopped. In 1798, when the creation of the Mississippi Territory officially signaled the end of Spanish authority in the area, the white population of the Natchez district had grown to 4,500, while blacks numbered some 2,400.

The assumption of territorial status marked the beginning of a new boom period in Mississippi. Over the next two decades a great migration occurred that resulted in the admission of two new states into the Union, Mississippi and Alabama. During these years Americans from the original states, especially Virginia, the Carolinas, and Georgia, were drawn to the new country by the powerful magnets of rich land and the promise of a better life. The praise which the British had heaped on Mississippi during the period 1763–1783 was, if anything, surpassed by that offered up by the Americans. Mississippi was variously hailed as the "Garden of America," the "Acadia of Southern America" where "soft zephyrs gently breathe on sweets, and the inhaled air gives a voluptuous glow of health and vigor, that seems to ravish the intoxicated senses."[7] The optimism and hopefulness of the new wave of settlers was articulated by the Maryland emigrant who said of his new Mississippi home: "The crops [here] are certain and want of the necessities of life never for a moment causes the heart to ache—abundance spreads the table of the poor man, and contentment smiles on every countenance."[8]

This idyllic view of the new Canaan may have been held by many white settlers, but it certainly was not held by blacks, who were brought into Mississippi in large numbers. Much of the impetus for the heavy migration into Mississippi after 1798 stemmed from the spread of cotton culture, made possible by Whitney's invention of the cotton gin, and the emergence of the Cotton Kingdom. Cotton culture rested squarely on slave labor, without which, as Robert Jenkins shows in his essay, "Africans in Colonial and Territorial Mississippi," there could have been no great Mississippi planter aristocracy. African Americans played a central role in shaping the early history of Mississippi. Indeed, Jenkins and the other contributors to this volume all point to the obvious fact that Mississippi was shaped by many influences. African Americans, Native Americans, Spanish, French, English, and Americans converged in colonial Mississippi, and her history can best be understood as a series of complex and continuing interactions among different peoples and diverse cultures over a period of centuries.

NOTES

1. Daniel J. Boorstin, *The Discoverers: A History of Man's Search to Know His World and Himself* (New York: Random House, 1983), 215.

2. Cecil Johnson, *British West Florida, 1763–1783* (New Haven: Yale University Press, 1943), 7–14.

3. Quoted in *ibid.*, 64–65.

4. *Ibid.*, 137–38; Bernard Bailyn, *Voyagers to the West: A Passage in the Peopling of America on the Eve of the Revolution* (New York: Knopf, 1986), 480.

5. Eron O. Rowland, "Peter Chester, Third Governor of the Province of British West Florida Under British Dominion, 1770–1781," *Publications of the Mississippi Historical Society*, 5 (1925), 67, 77.

6. Quoted in Bailyn, *Voyagers to the West*, 486. See also Johnson, *British West Florida*, and Albert C. Bates, ed., *The Two Putnams: Israel and Rufus in the Havana Expedition 1762 and in the Mississippi River Exploration 1772–73 with Some Account of the Company of Military Adventurers* (1932) for an account of Connecticut migration.

7. Gilbert Imlay, *A Topographical Description of the Western Territory of North America* (1792), 39; Samuel R. Brown, *The Western Gazetteer: or Emigrant's Directory* (1817), 15.

8. *Niles' Register*, XIII, 38.

The European Background
in the Late Fifteenth Century

Paul E. Hoffman

The Europe that Christopher Columbus left in his wake in August, 1492, still bore the outlines of the late Middle Ages. Its human landscape was marked by a rich cultural[1] diversity that included not only the language communities that are the bases for the modern nation states but also great variety in regional and even local cultures within those larger communities. Politically, economically, socially, religiously and intellectually, and artistically this was a menu from which only selected elements were to cross the world's oceans in the wake of Christopher Columbus's and Vasco da Gama's ships. Europeans could not help but transport fundamental things like systems and styles of government, economic habits, and social structures and values, although even these were to be transformed (or reformed) for the journey. Less fundamental things were selectively carried abroad. The pages that follow contain a brief overview of this varied Europe from which the explorers, conquerors, and colonizers of the Americas came.

Political

The political geography of Europe was only partially like that of our own time. In the west, the kingdoms of England, Scotland, Portugal, and France oc-

Above and opposite: These two maps, one ten years prior to Columbus's first voyage and one fifteen years after the voyage, indicate the immense change in perspective on the earth's size and shape in just one quarter of a century. Photographs by Richard Hurley. Maps courtesy of John Carter Brown Library, Brown University, Providence, Rhode Island. *Above:* 1482 German woodcut map of the world when most of Africa and Asia remain to be explored and the New World is as yet undreamed of.

cupied areas approximately the same as they do today.[2] What are today the states of Belgium and the United Netherlands was then the remnant of the Duchy of Burgundy, whose duke still owed homage to the King of France, at least in theory. "Spain" existed because Isabela of Castile was married to Ferdinand of Aragon, but in other respects these kingdoms were separate. Their eventual union under Juana I and then Charles I depended on accidents of inheritance that could not be foreseen in 1492 but that Ferdinand had prepared by his use of his and Isabela's children's marriages to circle France with his allies.[3] In Italy, the largest political unit was the Kingdom of Naples

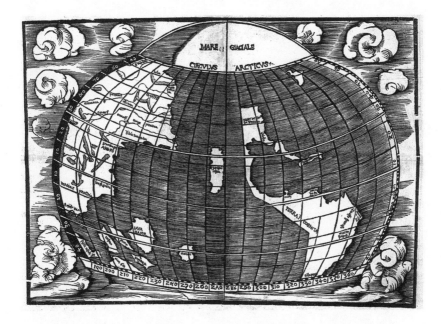

Jan Stobniczy copied this hemisphere from a Martin Waldseemuller map and published it in Krakow in 1507.

and Sicily, already a source of dispute (and war after 1494) between Charles VIII (and later Louis XI) of France and Ferdinand of Aragon, both of whom claimed it by right of biological descent from its previous ruling family. In the north, a congeries of city-states and principalities divided the land into a mosaic of small political units, many of which had come under the control of particular noble families, such as the Sforzas in Milan. In the center of the peninsula, the Papal States were ruled from Rome by the reputed successors of St. Peter.[4] The Swiss cantons formed a loose confederation of cities and rural areas tucked into the folds of the Alps.[5]

Central, eastern, and northern Europe were dominated by four empires: the Holy Roman Empire, which stretched from west of the Rhine River to east of the Oder River and from the Baltic Sea south to the Alps and the frontier with the Ottoman empire in Hungary; the Ottoman Empire, which was expanding by conquering more and more of the Balkans and Hungary[6]; the rapidly

The marriage in 1469 of Ferdinand of Aragon and Isabela of Castile assured the eventual unification of most of the Iberian peninsula, though each reigned as monarch in his or her own right. From a bas-relief in the Royal Chapel in Granada.

disintegrating Polish-Lithuanian empire which once had stretched from the Baltic almost to the Black Sea and held at least nominal control over the area of the modern republics of Poland, Lithuania, Byelorussia, and the Ukraine[7]; and the Danish Empire, which controlled not only the territory that today bears that name but also the areas of modern Norway, Sweden, Finland, and Iceland.[8] Estonia, Latvia, and parts of what is now Russia and Poland were governed by the Teutonic Knights. Farther east, the duchy of Muscovy was beginning to expand its authority in the territory that is now the eastern part of the Russian Republic.[9] Except for the Danish empire, which broke up in the sixteenth century, several centuries would pass before the collapse of these empires created states as linguistically and culturally coherent as the western European monarchies were in 1492.

The political systems of European states were of all sorts. In England, the medieval parliament remained strong, thanks in part to the recently-ended Wars of the Roses that had brought the Tudor line to the throne but had weakened the monarchy, at least temporarily. By custom, not only the nobility but also the owners of small farms were represented.[10] And uniquely in Europe, the principal seat of the royal court and of the parliament (i.e. the capital city) was also the largest city and principal port of the kingdom. This fact gave merchants a voice in government often denied them in other states, excepting the northern provinces of the Low Countries where merchant elites dominated the major cities and shared power with landed nobles in the Staats General, or parliament.

Elsewhere in Europe, parliamentary bodies were weaker and less representative. Frequently only certain cities enjoyed the right to send representatives to the body, and there was no tradition of elections of representatives by property holders. A few monarchs, and even some petty princes, were beginning to adopt Roman Law for their courts and with it ideas about their own rights as sovereigns to make the law without the consent of parliaments. They were also beginning to build bureaucratic administrative structures that relied on men educated in the new legal traditions and drawn from the lesser nobility and from the urban elites. This process was well advanced in Castile and somewhat less so in France, although in both the monarchs of the 1490s were still careful to call their parliamentary bodies into session in order to obtain new taxes and support for various reforms of government and law that strengthened the crown's powers over subjects not under seigniorial jurisdiction.[11] France and Castile thus foreshadowed developments that would appear in other states during the sixteenth and seventeenth centuries. Uniquely, Ferdinand and Isabela employed a council and viceroy system for governing Aragon. This method was later exported as the system for governing Spain's American colonies.

A more typical form of government was the sort of semi-confederation of monarch and subjects found in its most extreme forms in the Holy Roman Empire and the Kingdom of Poland. The Imperial Diet was an assemblage of princes great and small, free cities, and churchmen who were also territorial lords. The emperor had limited powers and was elected by the seven electors. His real power base was his own kingdom of Austria and his position as King of the Romans, the grand title of the ruler of Bohemia, the home of the Czech peoples.[12] The kingdom of Poland also was ruled by an elected monarch who had to deal with a parliamentary body divided by regional and family rivalries. Only in the Ottoman Empire did the ruler possess something akin to absolute (or unlimited) power, although that power was used in traditional ways.

Whatever the form of government, all monarchs were said to hold their powers from God for the purposes of maintaining some degree of order and justice within the society they ruled, for defending it against foreign enemies, and for achieving their own glory and the prosperity of their subjects by engaging successfully in war, usually to right some alleged wrong done to them (or their subjects) or to claim a disputed inheritance. Thus, in some respects, the states of Europe were still the medieval warrior kingdoms. On the frontiers of eastern Europe, the violence was more or less continuous. Further west, it ebbed and flowed in formal wars often fought by allies united by marriage as well as common interests. In Spain, a war of conquest against the Muslim kingdom of Granada was reviving crusader traditions. Permanent diplomatic representation existed only among the Italian city-states, and then primarily for intelligence-gathering purposes.[13]

Below the level of "national" governments, nobles and some cities often held nearly sovereign power over local districts. In each case, this semi-sovereignty rested on a granted or claimed right to administer justice within the district, and usually also the rights to collect taxes, to tax in limited ways, and generally to prevent the interference of royal agents in local matters. These seigniorial (if held by nobles) or civil jurisdictions (if held by towns) reflected the earlier medieval feudal arrangements. As monarchs began to gather power, they sought methods of reducing the independence of these vassals, limiting (but not necessarily replacing) their authority at the local level with that of agents not rooted in the district as property owners and long-term lords. In short, although kings might claim to be sovereign over all of a territory, in fact they often directly governed only a small fraction of it. In provinces of Castile, that fraction was as little as forty percent of the area and population.

The Economy

Just as the political geography of Europe bore only slight resemblance to that of today and was characterized by a high degree of regionalism and very weak central authority, so too the regional economies of Europe were only roughly joined together by long-distance trade and banking. The medieval centers in the Low Countries and in the port cities of Northern Italy maintained their historic roles as centers of manufacture and of exchange and distribution along the sea lanes, rivers, and overland routes that bound them to each other and to other cities and lesser towns, each in turn a center for commerce reaching into the more remote parts of their local regions.[14] But of these two centers, that in the Low Countries was the more important thanks to improvements in ship design and size that made it possible to trade across the length of the North and the Baltic seas, to England, and south to the Iberian Peninsula, the Senegal and Congo rivers in western Africa, the Atlantic Islands (Azores, Madeira, Canaries, Cape Verdes), and into the Mediterranean to Italy, as well as up the Rhine and other rivers that flowed to the North and Baltic seas from the populous interior of northern Europe. This growing maritime linkage of most of Europe to the Low Countries and nearby areas, often called the "commercial revolution" in textbooks, was rapidly eclipsing the economic importance of the overland route from the northern Italian cities to the cities of the Low Countries, a route that went around Switzerland and parallel to the Rhine.[15]

The forging of these maritime links carried with it the development of economic dependencies as areas outside of these two core economic zones increasingly exported primary goods, which were finished in the core areas and then returned as finished goods worth many times what the primary goods had sold for. In regional markets closely linked to this new system because they were centered on a seaport, for example Andalucía in southern Spain, local manufactures, especially textiles, were being driven out of the market. Textiles and other manufactured goods from nearby inland regional economies faced strong competition.[16] The merchants who engaged in foreign commerce, themselves often foreigners, generally did not invest profits in the industries of countries or regions that hosted them, preferring instead to

Early fifteenth-century woodcut of spice and grain merchants.

make money in commerce and to favor producers in their home areas (if they
were foreigners). The Genoese, whose merchant colonies could be found
throughout the Mediterranean, even in the Ottoman Empire, and whose
representatives traveled to northern Europe with cargos, were typical of these
merchants.[17] Dutch, English, and French merchants were beginning to settle
in small colonies in many ports in northern and even Mediterranean Europe,
although most of their presence in the Mediterranean trades was still on a
voyage-by-voyage basis.[18] The warrior nobles who controlled many governments and local areas and had contempt for the craftsmen and merchants of
the towns often paid little attention to the nationality of merchants or the fate
of local craft production. Displacements of local merchants by foreigners and
of local production by foreign goods thus could take place, to the detriment of
the long-term economic development of areas outside of the cores. In the
1490s, this process was only just beginning.

   Not only was this net of maritime and land communications forging the
patterns of dependency sometimes described as the "modern world system"

(which ended with World War II),[19] it also carried a monetized economy subject to the same sorts of inflationary and business cycle fluctuations as are found in our own times, if on a much smaller scale.[20] For persons only marginally touched by this system, or newly introduced into it, these fluctuations and the poverty or riches to be made from them seemed little more than the work of evil, greedy men. The taking of interest, a common feature of the system, was thought to be contrary to biblical and church teachings, although Italian churchmen had found ways to justify interest as early as the fourteenth century.[21] So, too, the developing market in real estate in many places—with a resulting tendency toward the concentration of land in the hands of fewer families—was often viewed as an evil by those unable to hold on to land.

Merchants provided banking, monetary exchange, and credit services over long distances, services that governments would discover and exploit in the next century. The Italians pioneered many of these developments, including double entry bookkeeping.[22]

This monetized and pan-European economy had an influence that dropped off rapidly as one moved away from the main cities and towns and trade routes. For most Europeans, including most peasants who farmed the land and lived in villages, economic activities were carried out in kind, however much values might be calculated in units of account. These rural Europeans, even more than those who lived in the towns, lived in an economy of scarcity and in an economic and social world defined by their families and villages and region.

The fundamental scarcity arose because harvests depended on the vagaries of weather, soils, attacks of plant diseases and insects, the customary frequency of crop rotation, and the amount of human labor expended in raising the crops.[23] Although grains and plant and animal sources of proteins were sometimes transported long distances by sea or river or on land to feed towns, most were consumed where they were produced by persons who had little money with which, during a time of scarcity, to purchase replacements from a distance. Moreover, the range of grains and plant sources for protein was limited because the Americas had not as yet been discovered, a development that was later to bring maize, potatoes, and a host of protein-rich beans to rural Europe.[24]

To this fundamental scarcity based in agriculture were added others arising from the limits imposed by the muscle power of animals and men in most other economic activities. Water wheels, windmills, and simple lever devices made some work lighter in some places, but mining, metallurgy, and the hand making of cloth, ceramics, and leather goods depended primarily on muscular sources of energy.

In such a world of scarcity, the expansion of the store of goods usually came at a human cost, made all the higher by the expansion of populations that was taking place in the late fifteenth century. Plundering during war was but the most extreme example of how a few could enrich themselves at the expense of others. Many other forms of "plunder"—taxation, tithes, seigniorial dues, even fraud—were used by the powerful to gather wealth from the laboring mass of their social inferiors, who in turn stole when no other means of survival was available. This activity probably took place across defined if not always clear lines between "us" and "them."[25]

Society

Broad definition of the "other" or the alien human group went hand in hand with the confining existence of the village and its region. Except for soldiers, and sailors in the coastal areas, few ordinary people ever traveled very far from their village unless it was to move to another village. Family and local community, often reinforced by local dialects and customs of dress that would be mocked in other places, drew a tight circle around "us" and so put many others into the "them" category. Religion reinforced this egocentrism by its vague stories of peoples hostile to the True Faith.

Village life was characterized not only by this high degree of social control and isolation but also by demographic patterns that had changed hardly at all for centuries. A third or more of the population was under the age of ten, the result of high fertility rates per marriage and equally high death rates among infants and small children. First marriages for men usually came late (in their late twenties) and might be followed by several marriages, each, like the first, lasting only a few years before a wife died in childbirth or from some other cause. Women married at younger ages, often to older men who had children and, more importantly, the resources to support a family. For young men, the relative dearth of brides of their own age and their own lack of control over economic assets meant that migration to a town or into the army or to sea were attractive alternatives to lives of poverty and sexual abstinence in the village. Women who survived the childbearing years usually lived to an old age in which there were fewer and fewer men of comparable longevity. That is, the demographic pattern among persons over thirty-five was not unlike our own except that far fewer persons lived to reach that age. Life expectancy at birth in most of Europe was under twenty-five years! It rose sharply as one got older, to about seventy years if one lived to be twenty-five.[26] Such dismal prospects aside, the villages of many parts of Europe were producing slightly more births than deaths in the late fifteenth century. In many, the demographic mass that had been lost because of the plague had long since been made up.

Towns and cities had different social structures and different demographic patterns from those found in villages. Some smaller towns still preserved the "commune" of craftsmen and professionals that had been the ideal in the later middle ages. Most were marked by social stratification caused by the presence of nobles and a few families that had grown rich through trade or by lending money. In some cities, such as those in northern Italy, these powerful families had come to monopolize public office and to dominate the religious confraternities around which so much social life revolved.[27] At a different level, older men dominated households organized around the craft specialties that, with trade, gave the towns their economic power over the surrounding countryside.[28]

Demographically the towns and cities were marked by constant immigration, maintaining or increasing their size by this process. Sanitary conditions were so bad that few urban populations, unlike those of the villages, could reproduce themselves. Consequently the towns had larger numbers of young people (late teens and older), especially young men, and fewer small children than villages did. As in the villages, older men in the towns often got their pick of younger women, creating social tensions with the younger men that were relieved by rituals and festivals that allowed the expression of pent-up aggressions.[29]

Social attitudes were often cruel in these small, localized societies in which material life was difficult. Scarcity and early death were pervasive aspects of life and seem to have produced in the population a certain detachment from the sufferings of others. In some unfortunate areas, the ravages of armies on the march were also recurring constants, although most European villages were touched by war only when the recruiting officer or the requisitioning agent came through. Banditry plagued some rural areas. The powerful, or the merely well-armed and violence-prone, could and did act oppressively toward ordinary people, often without suffering any legal consequences. Agonizing human deaths from injuries and illnesses for which there were few remedies and few anesthetics, except alcohol, accustomed people to detached observation of suffering. Such sport as there was involved pitting animals against each other (cock and dog fights) or torturing them (bear baiting). Even religion regularly celebrated a human sacrifice, with the "body" and "blood" of the victim at least symbolically consumed by one or more of the participants in the ritual. The social prestige associated with warriors also helped to reinforce this hard edge to European culture.

Europeans did not resort to the sort of crude ethnocentrism that defined other peoples as less than human, but they were prepared to act as if persons not of their group (village, region, army, sometimes even lineage) counted for less than themselves. Love, religious teachings about duty to neighbor, and a host of social conventions moderated this behavior within the communities from which the individual drew his/her identity and sometimes moderated it towards outsiders as well. On the whole, however, ordinary Europeans were suspicious and contemptuous of the "other" and prepared to treat the "other" in ways not used with the "us."

Religious and Intellectual Vigor

On the surface, Western Christendom was united in religious practice and governed in spiritual matters by the Pope at Rome. The Roman church had left the Great Schism of the fourteenth century behind after the meeting of the Council of Constance in 1417 and had driven the few remaining Lollards underground in England. The Hussites had won terms that allowed them to practice their version of Christianity in Bohemia.[30] However, the central administrative problems of the church, the granting of papal dispensations and the powerlessness of the bishops to control the monastic clergy in their sees, had not been resolved. Sales of office, holdings of multiple offices and the resulting absenteeism, and scandalous failures to abide by the rules of monastic orders flourished under the restored papacy, which was deeply involved in the political storms of Renaissance Italy and not very interested in the complaints of the pious.[31]

Within the seeming unity of western Christianity, a rich variety of beliefs and practices existed, especially those beliefs and practices that stressed individual, direct communion with the divine. Perhaps the best known were the practical mysticism of the Brethren of the Common Life (a lay movement in the Low Countries and the western provinces of the Holy Roman Empire) and the zealous reforming of the observants within the monastic orders, espe-

The pervasive influence of the church is clearly indicated in the title of the text
from which this illustration is taken—"The Art of Living and Dying Well"—
from baptism to final rites.

This page from the *Chronicle of Milan* (1503) presents a portrait of the author, Bernardino Cario, in an elaborately decorated frame, complete with moral sentiments. The manuscripts, inkwell and quill, and candle are typical accouterments of the scholar.

cially the Franciscans (notably in Castile). The latter, and many others, had various sorts of millenarian expectations quite at variance with the general stance and doctrine of the church as a whole. Everywhere localized cults of saints flourished along with general anti-Semitism and variably intense devotion to the Blessed Virgin. In more remote rural communities, vestiges of pre-Christian religious beliefs and practices could be found mixed in with more orthodox practices.[32]

Adding yet additional richness and variety to the whole were the on-going debates between the Thomists, the Platonists, and the Nominalists who occupied chairs in the philosophy faculties of the better universities such as Oxford, Paris, and Padua.[33] Humanist philosophers, who were adding yet more richness to the debate at Padua (for example) were not commonly found outside of Italy. The most important in 1492 were the Florentine Neo-Platonists.[34] However, the scholarly techniques and interest in ancient texts that were part of the humanist perspective could be found in places like Castile, where Cardinal Ximenez de Cisneros was at work on his famous Polyglot Bible. In short, this was a rich theological as well as philosophical time when religious intolerance had not yet silenced divergent voices within the mainstream or the fringes of theological debate.

Adding to the richness, texts of classical authors and church fathers were being printed on paper with moveable type in standardized editions, usually in the original languages but sometimes in translations into vernacular tongues such as French.[35] As more and more classical works were printed, they added information and points of view to earlier knowledge, challenging practitioners of the Scholastic method to virtuoso performances of their intellectual exercise of proving that all ancient authorities really spoke about a singular body of Truths. Renaissance intellectuals, as yet still found mostly in Italy, drew other conclusions from these new intellectual resources.

The Arts

Painters and sculptors of talent, like printers, were as yet few and mostly concentrated in the core areas of the European economy. Painting in oils, the use of perspective, dissection and the study of human anatomy, and techniques for creating light and shadow had been mastered in the century before 1492 and were well known to artists in both the Low Countries and Italy.[36] In Italy, Botticelli (1444–1510), Leonardo da Vinci (1452–1519), Raphael (1483–1520),

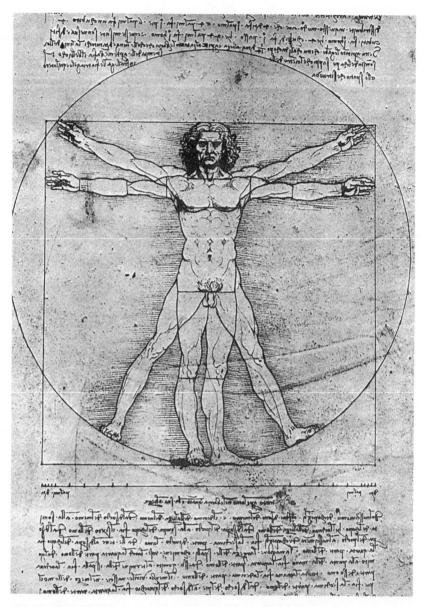

This familiar drawing by Leonardo da Vinci of the human body with limbs extended, within a circle and square, has become a standard symbol of the humanist concerns of the Renaissance, as expressed by a man and artist of genius.

the Venetian school (e.g., Titian, c. 1477–1576) and the young Michelangelo (1475–1564) were defining the high Renaissance tradition of painting. Donatello had died thirty years earlier, but his tradition of sculpture continued, heavily inspired both by Greek statuary and by studies of anatomy. The Flemish school that had introduced oil painting early in the fifteenth century was still flourishing, led by Hans Memling (ca. 1430–1494), but the greatest age of Flemish painting lay ahead. Elsewhere in Europe, medieval aesthetics dominated in sculpture (mostly for churches) and painting, although the new styles were being introduced wherever the pan-European trading system was well established.

Folk music, like almost every other aspect of village life, was highly varied. Folk songs had many forms, some derived from medieval plain song, some from ballads, some from other traditions of often ancient origins. Drums and flute-like wind instruments could be found almost everywhere, usually paired to accompany dancing. Other forms of wind instruments, such as trumpets and reed instruments, were used in towns and the courts of the wealthy. Churches in towns of any size usually had a small pump organ to accompany the Mass. Plucked or strummed stringed instruments based on the lute were also popular. Ancestral forms of the modern guitar could be found in the Iberian peninsula. Formal composition of songs and more elaborate musical forms was confined to the households of a few wealthy patrons. There the dominant musical forms were the motet, invented earlier in Italy, and early polyphonic works. The Ducal court of Burgundy was a center of musical innovation.[37]

Literature in the form of novels was in its infancy, but its many other forms were well represented: storytelling, the repetition of ballads and romances, the writing of often elaborate poems, plays, and various forms of prose were common. Formal writing was often still in Latin, with heavy classical influences in cities touched by the Renaissance. Petrarch's poetry inspired many imitators in Italy. A few prose versions of the chivalric romance had begun to appear in Italian vernacular, but the poetic form was more typical. Epics and very personal ruminations on life, both inspired by classical examples or cast in classical forms, and sometimes incorporating themes from the romances, flowed from many pens.

Medieval theatrical traditions were still strong. Farces, sacred themes, and comedy graced stages at courts and in town squares. Spectacle was especially important in plays presented at courts. Classical plays by Plautus and Terence were performed in Latin and inspired new works, often in vernacular, at least in Italy. Elsewhere the impact of the classics was negligible.

Annals and accounts of great events were commonly in prose but often also took poetic form. Works of moral instruction or popularized philosophical ideas were important parts of the prose writing of the time. The Italian *novella* was widely circulated there; the works of popular authors such as Masuccio Salernitano were collected and published.

In general, however, the further west and north from Italy, the more medieval the literary and dramatic forms. Lyric poetry, romances, chronicles in verse, sagas, and similar rhymed forms continued, if with increasingly formalized styles that critics of the sixteenth century found wanting. Religious plays were more common. To the east and north, Latin traditions faded into those coming from Byzantium, except for the few Polish nobles who had been educated in Renaissance Italy and carried home its literary forms.

Such then was the diversity of Europe seen as a whole. This large-scale diversity was multiplied many times over on the local scale, to the point that some scholars are reluctant to write about anything but a town or region. Yet this rich diversity was slowly being drawn into a single pan-European culture made possible by the printing press and long-distance trade, which included books. The exploration and colonization of the New World, when it came, detached individuals and groups of kin from their local cultural settings and brought them together in ways that would have been impossible in Europe except among armies or in the major port cities. Necessarily, the culture(s) these immigrants carried with them included some of the best, and worst, features of late fifteenth-century Europe. In the new world created by the voyages of Columbus and Da Gama, these Europeans of limited horizons often failed to handle unprecedented circumstances (such as meeting peoples with simple cultures) with the grace and charity their descendants might wish. Yet we do them, and ultimately ourselves, a disservice if we fail to learn about and better understand their humanity.

Notes

1. Culture is here used in its most inclusive sense to denote all aspects of human behavior and belief and the material objects used by or created by humans.
2. There are many histories of France and England that cover this period both

generally and in detail. For Portugal, Harold V. Livermore, *A History of Portugal* (Cambridge: Cambridge University Press, 1947) remains a good short treatment.

3. John H. Elliott, *Imperial Spain, 1469–1716* (London: Edward Arnold, 1963), 1–134, is an excellent introduction to "Spain" in this period.

4. Lauro Martines, *Power and Imagination; City-States in Renaissance Italy* (New York: Alfred E. Knopf, 1979) and Denys Hay and John Law, *Italy in the Age of the Renaissance* (New York: Longman, 1989) are good discussions of late fifteenth-century Italy.

5. G. E. Potter, *A Short History of Switzerland* (Oxford: Clarendon Press, 1952) provides brief coverage. See also William D. McCrackan, *Rise of the Swiss Republic* (New York: Henry Holt, 2nd ed.; 1901), which, in spite of its age, is still a useful survey.

6. The Ottoman empire is not well studied in English, but see Paul Coles, *The Ottoman Impact on Europe* (New York: Harcourt, Brace & World, 1968) for an introduction and *Cambridge History of Islam*, Part III (Cambridge: Cambridge University Press), and *New Cambridge Modern History*, vol. 1, Chapter 14 (Cambridge: Cambridge University Press).

7. George E. Slocombe, *A History of Poland* (London: T. Nelson and Sons, Ltd., rev. ed.; 1939) is an early survey in English. Better is Norman Davies, *God's Playground: A History of Poland, vol. 1, Origins to 1795* (New York: Columbia University Press, 1981). For the Ukraine, see William E. D. Allen, *The Ukraine, a History* (Cambridge: Cambridge University Press, 1940).

8. Stewart P. Oakley, *The Story of Denmark* (London: Faber, 1972) is the best short history in English. For Norway, see Thomas K. Derry, *A Short History of Norway* (London: Allen & Unwin, 1957), 68–88. For Sweden, see Christiane I. Andersson, *A History of Sweden* (English translation, New York: Praeger, 1956). Eino Jutikkala, *A History of Finland* (New York: Praeger, 1962) briefly covers this period.

9. George Vernadsky, *The Origins of Russia* (Oxford: Clarendon Press, 1959) covers not only Russia but also its western neighbors. Michael T. Florinsky, *Russia, A History and Interpretation* (New York: Macmillan, 2 vols; 1953), vol. 1, is considered by many to be the best narrative in English of these early developments. For a study of frontiers, see James H. Bater and R. A. French, *Studies in Russian Historical Geography* (New York: Academic Press, 1983).

10. Howard L. Gray, *The Influence of the Commons on Early Legislation* (Cambridge: Harvard University Press, 1932) traces the growth of the lower house's power. Also useful are E. F. Jacob, *The Fifteenth Century, 1399–1485* (Oxford: Clarendon Press, 1969) and J. D. Mackie, *The Early Tudors, 1485–1558* (Oxford: Clarendon Press, 1952).

11. Elliott, *Imperial Spain*, 78, 81.

12. Francis L. Carstein, *Princes and Parliaments in Germany From the Fifteenth to the Eighteenth Century* (Oxford: Clarendon Press, 1959) is a good introduction to the history of the Holy Roman Empire and its institutions.

13. Garrett Mattingly, *Renaissance Diplomacy* (London: Cape, 1955) is the classic study of the beginnings of modern diplomacy.

14. For economic developments in general, see selected essays in *The Cambridge Economic History of Europe* (New York: Cambridge University Press) vols. 1–3; for the trade routes see John H. Parry, "Transport and Trade Routes," in vol. 4, *The Economy of Expanding Europe in the Sixteenth and Seventeenth Centuries*, ed. E. E. Rich and C.H. Wilson (Cambridge: Cambridge University Press, 1967), 155–222. H. Van der Wee, *The Growth of the Antwerp Market and the European Economy* (The Hague: Nijhoff, 1963) is also useful.

15. H. A. Miskimin, *Economy of Early Renaissance Europe* (Englewood Cliffs, N.J.: Prentice-Hall, 1969) is an overview. Carlo M. Cipolla, *Guns, Sails, and Empires* (New York: Minerva, 1965), discusses the technological innovations that made long distance voyaging and conquest possible. Eva G. K. Taylor, *The Haven-Finding Art* (New York: Abelard-Schuman, 1957), chapters 5–7, is a classic study of navigational techniques at this time.

16. These dynamics in the markets of Seville are partially described by Ruth Pike, *Enterprise and Adventure, the Genoese in Seville and the Opening of the New World* (Ithaca: Cornell University Press, 1966). For a later date, see Stanley and Barbara Stein, *Colonial Heritage of Latin America; Essays on Economic Dependence in Perspective* (New York: Oxford University Press, 1970), 46–52.

17. Felipe Fernandez Armesto, *Before Columbus; Exploration and Colonization From the Mediterranean to the Atlantic 1229–1492* (Philadelphia: University of Pennsylvania Press, 1987), 96–120, describes the Genoese commercial empire of the later middle ages.

18. Gordon Connell-Smith, *Forerunners of Drake, A Study of English Trade with Spain in the Early Tudor Period* (London: Published for the Royal Empire Society by Longmans, 1954), discusses the English in Andalucía.

19. Immanuel Wallerstein, *The Modern World System* (3 vols.; New York: Academic Press, 1974–1988) is a comprehensive, if not always comprehensible, description of the system. Volume 3 carries the story to 1840.

20. For a brief history of prices from 1450 onwards, see Fernand Braudel, "Prices in Europe from 1450 to 1750," in *The Cambridge Economic History of Europe*, 4:378–486.

21. Benjamin Nelson, *The Idea of Usury* (Princeton: Princeton University Press, 1949) examines this topic in depth.

22. Richard Ehrenberg, *Capital and Finance in the Age of the Renaissance*, trans. H. M. Lucas (New York: Harcourt, 1928), is a detailed study of the Fugger banking firm. Other details of banking, exchange, and credit can be found in *Cambridge Economic History of Europe*, vol. 2.

23. Fernand Braudel, *Civilization and Capitalism 15th-18th Centuries, I, The Structures of Everyday Life*, trans. Sian Reynolds (New York: Harper & Row, 1981); *Cambridge Economic History of Europe*, vol. 1.

24. Alfred E. Crosby, *The Columbian Exchange: Biological and Cultural Consequences of 1492* (Westport, Conn.: Greenwood Publishing Company, 1972), 165–207.

25. Natalie Z. Davis, *The Return of Martin Guerre* (Cambridge: Harvard University Press, 1983), explores some of the dynamics of the "us" and "them" in a southern French village while discussing an unusual case of impersonation that was made into an award-winning French movie.

26. Peter Laslett, *The World We Have Lost: Further Explored* (3rd ed.; New York: Scribner's, 1984), is a basic work on early-Modern demography. See also Michael W. Flinn, *The European Demographic System, 1500–1800* (Baltimore: Johns Hopkins University Press, 1981), for a slightly later period but whose general characteristics are found in 1492.

27. Edward Muir, *Civic Ritual in Renaissance Venice* (Princeton, N.J.: Princeton University Press, 1981), discusses confraternities and the use of rituals, among other things, related to this topic. More on confraternities is found in Ronald F. E. Weissman, *Ritual Brotherhood in Renaissance Florence* (New York: Academic Press, 1982), and Richard Trexler, *Public Life in Renaissance Florence* (New York: Academic Press, 1980).

28. George Huppert, *After the Black Death; A Social History of Early Modern Europe* (Bloomington: Indiana University Press, 1986) provides a rich examination of these sorts of social phenomena, although with a primary orientation to the sixteenth and later centuries, for which there is better information.

29. Huppert, *After the Black Death*, 37–40. An excellent analysis of the social consequences of the differences in ages between husbands and brides appears in David Herlihy and Christiane Klapisch-Zuber, *Tuscans and Their Families* (New Haven: Yale University Press, 1985). See also David Herlihy, *Medieval Households* (Cambridge: Harvard University Press, 1985).

30. Gordon Leff, *Heresy in the Later Middle Ages . . . c. 1250–c. 1450* (2 vols., New York: Barnes & Noble, 1967), is a general survey of all these movements. For a highly detailed account of the Hussites, see Howard Kaminsky, *A History of the Hussite Revolution* (Berkeley: University of California Press, 1967).

31. Of the many histories of the Catholic Church and the papacy, one of the better accounts of this period is Mandell Creighton, *A History of the Papacy From the Great Schism to the Sack of Rome* (6 vols., new ed.; London: Longmans, Green & Co., 1897).

32. For example, Carlo Ginzburg, *The Night Battles; Witchcraft, and Agrarian Cults in the Sixteenth and Seventeenth Centuries* (Baltimore: Johns Hopkins University Press, 1983), which describes an apparent fertility cult that survived in northern Italy into the sixteenth century.

33. Heiko A. Oberman, *The Harvest of Medieval Theology* (Cambridge: Harvard University Press, 1962), and Alister E. McGrath, *The Intellectual Origins of the European Reformation* (New York: B. Blackwell, 1987), discuss the traditions.

34. Charles E. Trinkaus, *The Scope of Renaissance Humanism* (Ann Arbor: University of Michigan Press, 1983), and Paul O. Kristeller, *Renaissance Thought: The Classic, Scholastic, and Humanist Strains* (New York: Harper & Row, 1961).

35. Elizabeth L. Eisenstein, *The Printing Press as an Agent of Change* (New York: Cambridge University Press, 1979) surveys this important development.

36. Erwin Panofsky, *Early Netherlandish Painting, Its Origins and Character* (2 vols.; Cambridge: Harvard University Press, 1953); Peter Murray and Linda Murray, *The Art of the Renaissance* (New York: Praeger, 1963); Otto Benesch, *The Art of the Renaissance in Northern Europe; Its Relation to the Contemporary Spiritual and Intellectual Movements* (rev. ed.; London: Phaidon Publishers, 1965); Bernard Berenson, *The Italian Painters of the Renaissance* (New York: Meridian Books, 1957), are among the many studies of these topics.

37. Gustave Reese, *Music in the Renaissance* (rev. ed.; New York: Norton, 1959) is the leading work on the topic.

SUGGESTED READINGS

Breisach, Ernst. *Renaissance Europe, 1300–1517* (New York: Macmillan, 1973) is a solid textbook treatment of the period.

Ferguson, Wallace K. *Europe in Transition: 1300–1520* (Boston: Houghton Mifflin, 1963) provides an overview of general social and economic conditions.

Cardini, Franco. *Europe 1492: Portrait of a Continent Five Hundred Years Ago* (New York: Facts on File, 1989) is also an overview.

Hale, John Rigby. *Renaissance Europe: The Individual and Society, 1480–1520* (New York: Harper & Row, 1972) discusses quality of life, not great events.

New Cambridge Modern History, vol. 1, *The Renaissance, 1493–1520* (Cambridge: Cambridge University Press, 1957–   ) has essays covering most of the topics noted herein in spite of the inclusive dates in its title.

European Interest
in the Gulf Coast, 1500–1699

Robert S. Weddle

As far as the written record goes, European interest in the Gulf coast of the present-day United States began in 1513, when Juan Ponce de León set out to discover Bímini and found Florida instead. His purpose probably was the taking of slaves rather than seeking the legendary Fountain of Youth. In the succeeding two centuries, the coast held an appeal for several nations, for diverse reasons, most of them related to economic opportunity. This interest was fed by a thirst for knowledge, but only in the sense that knowledge was the key to wealth and power. Concern for saving Indian souls motivated religious orders, usually with frustrating, if not disastrous, results. The Gulf's secluded bays and inlets, safe from storm and the watchful eyes of jealous Spaniards, provided refuge for a host of multinational freebooters, the true masters of Gulf navigation.

Identity of the first European to enter the Gulf of Mexico is as uncertain as are the names of those who may have reached America before Columbus. Following the Columbian voyages, mapmakers—beginning with Juan de la Cosa in 1500—portrayed a hypothetical land mass beyond Cuba that no known Euro-

Juan Ponce de León.

pean had yet seen. But only through the continuing process of discovery could the accuracy of such hypothecation be determined.

Prior to Ponce's voyage from Puerto Rico, another Spaniard, Sebastián de Ocampo, had discovered the Gulf in 1508–1509, while circumnavigating Cuba and proving its insularity. For several years thereafter, the Spaniards' interest focused on the southern Gulf. Francisco Hernández de Córdoba discovered Yucatán in 1517. Juan de Grijalva extended the discovery the following year to the southern and western Gulf coast as far as Cabo Rojo, thus revealing the riches of the Mejican (Aztec) empire. In 1519 Hernán Cortés began the conquest of Mexico.

Francisco de Garay, governor of Jamaica, meanwhile, heard of the unexplored territory between Ponce de León's discoveries and Grijalva's. He saw in the unknown region a potential antidote to the economic woes that afflicted his personal fortunes. With permission from the Crown's West Indies administrators, he sent four ships commanded by Alonso Alvarez de Pineda to search the unknown coast for a strait leading to the "South Sea," or Pacific Ocean. In disproving such a passage, Alvarez de Pineda produced the first map of the enclosed sea and provided the first description of its northern coast. He also proved Florida not an island, as Ponce had supposed, and discovered the Mississippi River.

After encountering Cortés's forces near Veracruz, Alvarez returned to the Río Pánuco—not the Río Grande or the Mississippi as has been claimed—which he had visited previously. He spent six weeks there before sailing homeward. The following year, he returned to the Pánuco to form a tenuous colony and lost his life in the Huastec uprising that destroyed it.

Neither Alvarez de Pineda's report to Garay nor Garay's to the Crown is known. Most of what is known of the voyage comes from the royal *cédula* granting Garay authority to settle the region explored, called Amichel, and the map sketch that was attached to it. None of the features described in the document—fertile lands, rivers yielding fine gold, and peaceful natives wearing gold jewelry, some dwarfs and others giants more than seven feet tall—is assigned to a specific location. Few place-names appear on the map. One that does is the Río del Espíritu Santo—the Mississippi—shown emptying into the Gulf through a small bay. Although the Gulf of Mexico's coastal configuration changed in response to new discoveries, this bay—except for a tendency to grow in successive representations—remained constant. Some maps labeled it Mar Pequeña ("Little Sea") or Bahía del Espíritu Santo—a misconception that was to confuse explorers.

The years that followed the Alvarez de Pineda voyage were marked by a string of disasters that dampened enthusiasm for occupying the coast. Ponce de León returned to the Florida peninsula with would-be settlers in 1521 but withdrew under Indian attack and shortly died of his wounds. Garay, seeking to revive the lost colony on the Río Pánuco in 1523, found that Cortés had already seized control. He himself died during a visit to Mexico City to treat with the conqueror. Pánfilo de Narváez, the loser in a confrontation with Cortés in 1520, won a royal concession for exploration and conquest "from the Río de las Palmas to the Island of Florida." Dreaming of finding another native kingdom as rich as Mexico, he landed on the Florida peninsula in April, 1528. Rumors of gold heard among the Indians spurred him on to Apalache, where he and his men escaped the first stages of disaster by building crude boats for sailing to Pánuco. Ultimately, these craft were scattered along the Texas shore from Galveston Bay to the Río Grande and beyond, their occupants—excepting only Alvar Núñez Cabeza de Vaca and three companions—slain by Indians.

As Narváez had glimpsed the wealth of Mexico, Hernando de Soto had tasted that of Peru. As Narváez had been thwarted in his dealings with Cortés,

Alonso de Santa Cruz's "Soto" map (mid-sixteenth century) reflecting expeditions of Juan Ponce de León, Lucas Vazquez de Ayllon, Pánfilo de Narváez, and Francisco Vazquez de Coronado, as well as Hernando de Soto's. Courtesy Barker Texas History Center, University of Texas at Austin.

Soto had been frustrated in Peru by the conflict between the Pizarros and the Almagros. He nevertheless could have lived out his days comfortably with his Peruvian loot. His interest in the Gulf coast, therefore, must be attributed to the conquistador spirit that caused him always to thirst for greater wealth and glory. But Florida was not Peru. Soto, on his march through nine southern states, lost his fortune and his life. Having chosen his *maestre de campo*, Luis de Moscoso Alvarado, to carry on, he was entombed in the waters of "a great river that is in the land, called Rio de Spiritu Santo"—the Mississippi. The river at last provided Moscoso's escape route, though by no means an easy one.

The military conquest of Florida, in three attempts, had signally failed. The next attempt, backed by the venerable Dominican bishop and champion of the American Indian, Bartolomé de las Casas, would seek to win the Florida natives with the Christian gospel. One of Las Casas's disciples, Fray Luis

Cáncer de Barbastro, in 1549 put together an expedition that included a Florida Indian brought to Mexico by Soto's men. The woman, who had professed Christianity, was to serve as interpreter. Cáncer, however, misjudged the firmness of her Christian commitment. What appears to have been her betrayal led to the martyrdom of Father Cáncer and two other members of his religious order on the Florida shore near Charlotte Harbor.

The Gulf coast thereafter suffered from "bad press." Contributing to its unfortunate reputation was the massacre of most of some 400 castaways from the 1554 wreck of three Spanish ships on Padre Island off the Texas coast. Influential persons began urging a settlement on the coast where ships beset by storm might seek shelter from the sea and refuge from hostile Indians. Among them was Rodrigo Ranjel, of late Hernando de Soto's secretary and now *alcalde mayor* of Pánuco, who advocated settlements at the Río de las Palmas, the Río Bravo (Río Grande), and Ochuse—Pensacola Bay. The New Spain viceroy, Luis de Velasco, at last sent three vessels commanded by Guido de Lavazares to explore the coast from the Río de las Palmas to the Florida peninsula. Lavazares, reaching Matagorda Bay in Texas in the fall of 1558, was driven off by contrary winds, to approach the coast again among the islands of Mississippi Sound. He explored Mobile Bay and continued east to a point beyond Choctawhatchee Bay. He was unable to enter Pensacola Bay, though it later became the primary site for the abortive colony headed by Tristán de Luna y Arellano, 1559–61.

The Luna *entrada* reflects Viceroy Velasco's intense interest in the northern Gulf coast. The high official had great expectations for Luna's accomplishments, hardly any of which were realized. He hoped that Luna would explore and sound the rivers emptying into the Gulf, south to the Florida Keys and west to the Mississippi, and link the colony with his planned overland expedition from Zacatecas. He visualized the extension of roads from the Mississippi to the Atlantic coast. He also expected a mine discovery. Luna's illness, affecting his ability to lead, seems to have voided such hopes. With Luna's disability apparent, Angel de Villafañe was sent to succeed him and move the colony to Santa Elena on the Atlantic coast. This effort also failed. In truth, Luna's illness was only partly to blame for his lack of success. The chief cause of the colony's failure may lie in Velasco's great desire to see it succeed. Distance rendered his personal control impossible, and his attempt to keep a tight rein undercut Luna's effectiveness.

Pedro Menéndez de Avilés, after founding St. Augustine in 1565, established a short-lived settlement called San Antonio on the Gulf side of the lower Florida peninsula, designed to guard the shipping lanes and rescue castaways. From his post at Santa Elena, in 1566 and 1567, Menéndez sent expeditions under Juan Pardo to "discover and conquer the interior from there to Mexico" through the country explored previously by Soto. Pardo's road to New Spain fell far short. Menéndez, taking the term "La Florida" in its broader context, asked for and got authority to settle the Gulf coast to the border with New Spain, near the Río Pánuco. But it was just another dream. At his death in 1574, nothing had been done to bring it to fruition. Luis de Carvajal y de la Cueva, to win colonization rights in northern Mexico and Texas, took up the cause of a Florida-Mexico link, but his promises far exceeded his performance; he was dedicated more to taking Indian slaves.

In 1597, Spanish Franciscans began to push across the Florida peninsula from St. Augustine to establish missions among the Timucua. By 1608 Father Martín Prieto advanced into Apalache territory, west of the Aucilla River, but a lack of missionaries stalled the effort. While Father Prieto struggled against the Crown's lack of commitment and the lingering hostility from Soto's *entrada*, the English established their first permanent American colony. By 1627 both the English and the Dutch were attempting to move into the vacuum that existed along the Gulf coast and north of the Florida frontier. English traders began stirring discontent among the Indians. By 1640 a Gulf port was opened at St. Marks to supply the missions. The post of San Luis de Apalache was established at Tallahassee's site in 1645. Ultimately, the mission chain extended, though feebly, "twelve leagues" west of the Apalachicola River, but scant knowledge accrued of the territory beyond that point.

Change was wrought by Robert Cavelier, Sieur de La Salle's descent of the Mississippi River in 1682 and his effort to plant a colony on the Gulf coast three years later—the first serious threat to Spanish domination in the Gulf of Mexico. La Salle envisioned a chain of French trading posts throughout the Mississippi Valley, served by a warm-water port that would be accessible when the Great Lakes and the St. Lawrence River were frozen. He also envisioned a post on the lower Mississippi that would serve the current war effort by harassing Spanish shipping and seizing the Mexican mines. His ships sailed into the "Spanish Sea" in January, 1685, without knowledge that the war with Spain had ended since he left France. The victim of the limited geographical knowledge of his times, La Salle landed where he had never meant to be—at Matagorda Bay in Texas. There his colony of three hundred succumbed to

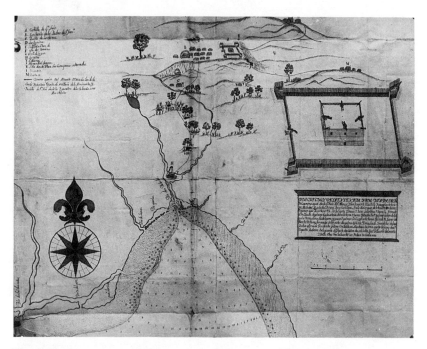

The Apalache posts established in mid-seventeenth century: San Marcos and San Luis and the road connecting them. Courtesy of Archivo General de Indias, Seville.

mismanagement, disease, and Indian trouble. La Salle himself died at the hands of his own men while trying to reach his post on the Illinois River. A Spanish expedition headed by General Alonso de León found the ruined settlement on Garcitas Creek near the head of Lavaca Bay in April, 1689, a few months after its final destruction by the Karankawa.

León's journey from Coahuila represented the climax of a Spanish search that had gone on for more than three years, by land and sea. Spanish ships had closely examined the coast between San Marcos de Apalache and Tampico, rediscovering Pensacola and Mobile bays and limning the Mississippi Delta. To thwart further intrusion, the Spaniards established in eastern Texas two missions of short duration. There followed a three-way race for mastery of the northern Gulf shore by France, Spain, and England. Spain, intimidated by the drift-laden torrent pouring from the Mississippi's mouth and lacking knowl-

Pensacola Bay and its new post of San Carlos de Austria, 1698. The cartouche
credits Andres de Arriola, but the map undoubtedly was the work of Jaime
Franck, the Austrian engineer who directed the building of fortifications. Courtesy of Barker Texas History Center, University of Texas at Austin.

edge of the river itself, chose to settle Pensacola Bay. It did so in 1698, ahead of
its rivals. By this time, however, both France and England were looking toward the great river of which they had knowledge stemming from La Salle's
exploration. It was La Salle's vision of mastering this vital waterway to create a
commercial empire that drove them.

  Pierre Le Moyne, Sieur d'Iberville, pursuing La Salle's dream, established in
1699 a French beachhead on Mississippi Sound and found his way into the
river mouth almost six months ahead of the English captain William Bond.
Bond was agent for Dr. Daniel Coxe's colonization scheme. Having first explored the coast a hundred leagues west of the Mississippi, he entered the river
on August 29, 1699, planning to rendezvous in Chickasaw country with
Carolina traders guided by the French renegade Jean Couture. He was turned
back by Iberville's 19-year-old brother, Jean Baptiste Le Moyne, Sieur de Bienville, at the bend in the river since known as English Turn.

  France thus gained control of the Mississippi. The Spanish post at Pensacola

The mouths of the Mississippi, drawn by Minet (La Salle's engineer), c. 1684. Courtesy of Public Archives of Canada, Ottawa.

Bay, too weak to object, was forced into a symbiotic partnership with the French to thwart the English. Within a year, Iberville saw the establishment of Fort Maurepas and exploration of much of the surrounding country. Reinforcements from France began a fort to guard the river and fanned out to extend French influence up the Mississippi valley. Spain's actions in the future would be governed largely by what the French did.

SUGGESTED READINGS

Galloway, Patricia K., ed. *La Salle and His Legacy: Frenchmen and Indians in the Lower Mississippi Valley.* Jackson: University Press of Mississippi, 1982.

Gannon, Michael V. *The Cross in the Sand. The Early Catholic Church in Florida, 1513–1870.* Gainesville: University Presses of Florida, 1965.

Hodge, Frederick W., and T.H. Lewis, eds. *Spanish Explorers in the Southern United States, 1528–1543.* New York: Scribner, 1907.

McWilliams, Richebourg Gaillard, trans. and ed. *Iberville's Gulf Journals.* University: University of Alabama Press, 1981.

Priestley, Herbert Ingram, trans. and ed. *The Luna Papers: Documents Relating to the Expedition of Don Tristán de Luna y Arellano for the Conquest of La Florida in 1559–1561.* 2 vols., 1928. Reprint. New York: Books for Libraries Press, 1971.

Weddle, Robert S. *Spanish Sea: The Gulf of Mexico in North American Discovery, 1500–1685.* College Station: Texas A&M University Press, 1985.

Weddle, Robert S., Mary Christine Morkovsky, and Patricia Galloway, eds., *La Salle, the Mississippi, and the Gulf: Three Primary Documents.* College Station: Texas A&M University Press, 1987.

European Colonization of Mississippi

William Cash

Numerous textbooks and even many history teachers initiate the American story with Jamestown. Such a starting point logically leads to an emphasis on the Anglo-American frontier. Thus, Spanish and French settlements are often ignored or relegated to the role of obstacles to the English westward movement. Indeed, some writers and teachers suggest that Mississippi has no colonial history, but only an Indian heritage prior to the arrival of English-speaking settlers.

This kind of Anglo-American frontier emphasis omits or relegates to a cursory survey a significant segment of Mississippi's history. Furthermore, such an emphasis has at times distorted treatment of the vicious international rivalry for political control in areas of present-day Mississippi. France, England, Spain, and finally the United States of America vied for control of the area, in war and diplomacy, until the contest was concluded by the Adams-Onis Treaty, 1819–1821. Unfortunately, the Anglo-American frontier emphasis details the contributions of but one of the participants to civilization of the United States. Notwithstanding their political ousters, France and Spain contributed significant components to the Mississippi heritage.

Juan Ponce de León, whose search for gold was spurred on by false tales of gold circulated by the Indians, began in 1513 the first recorded Spanish exploration in North America. León landed in an area that he named "La Florida." Although his efforts have been characterized by some as gullible and greedy, and thus unsuccessful, his optimistic report to the Spanish crown resulted in additional expeditions into the Gulf area.

In 1519, Alonso Alvarez de Pineda was sent in search of a strait leading from the Gulf of Mexico. Pineda found no strait but did map the entire northern coast of the Gulf from Florida to modern Mexico. His charts of the estuaries included the marking of the mouth of Río del Espíritu Santo, which we know as the Mississippi River. To his map he appended reports of gold ornaments worn by giant natives of the region. Pineda's was the first Spanish map in North America, and it included the Mississippi shore. Furthermore, his map and report stimulated subsequent explorations.[1]

Authorities debate the route of Pánfilo de Narváez's expedition, but historians universally acclaim the great significance of this exploration. In 1528, Narváez led a party from Spain to Tampa Bay and subsequently to the vicinity of Tallahassee. The men suffered severe deprivations and ultimately lost their ships. In an ingenious plan, the men killed their horses, built boats, and embarked on a route hugging the Gulf coast in an effort to get to New Spain. Authorities agree that their westward trek approximated the Pineda route, although no landing on the Mississippi shore has been documented. Narváez and most of the party were lost at sea, but Alvar Núñez Cabeza de Vaca and his small party continued their remarkable journey and eventually reached New Spain. Two significances of the Narváez-Vaca expedition relate to Mississippi. Initially, Vaca confirmed that the land mass to the north of Spanish settlements was a continent. Perhaps of more immediate significance, the glowing reports of the areas visited by Vaca prompted the almost simultaneous dual explorations of Francisco Coronado in the west and Hernando Soto in the east.[2]

Archaeologists and historians continue their research to mark the precise route of Soto through Mississippi. Place names coupled with early interpretations located extreme northern Mississippi as the probable route. More recent claims suggest a possible crossing of the Mississippi River as far south as Coahoma County. Largely the confusion results from a lack of discovery of material artifacts. Portable artifacts, which may have been carried far from their original sites by traders or others, create excitement but are not definitive, and the mobility of Indian tribes contributes to the controversies.

What is known is that Soto embarked on his voyage in 1539 and wandered

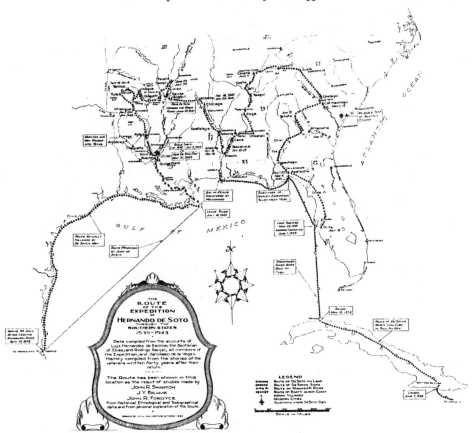

This 1932 Swanton map of the Soto expedition's route through the southeastern United States, 1539–1543, is contested in many of its details by contemporary historians and archaeologists. However, it does illustrate that Soto traversed the state of Mississippi, crossing the Tombigbee River near Columbus and reached the Mississippi River in June of 1541. His trail of destruction, from battles with the Indians to the lingering aftermath of disease, forever altered the native population and began the written history of the region. Courtesy of Mississippi Department of Archives and History.

for three years in at least nine and possibly eleven states in the Gulf coast region. All authorities agree that Soto traversed the entire breadth of Mississippi from east to west and reached and navigated the Mississippi River. Soto developed a fever, died, and was replaced by Luis de Moscoso Alvarado, who led the survivors to New Spain.

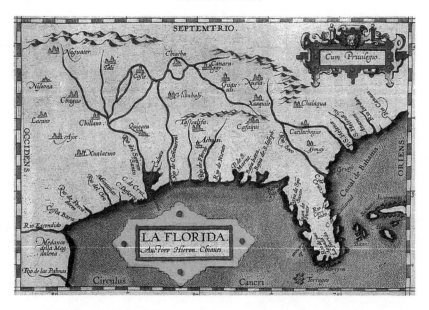

Map of "La Florida" by Hieronymus Chaves, dated 1545. This map drew upon new information about the interior of a portion of North America supplied by the Soto expedition. Courtesy of University of South Florida Special Collections.

Interestingly, Soto's body was shrouded in furs and deposited in the Mississippi River. Herein lies the tragedy that befell a man seeking instant wealth.

The rich fur-bearing region he explored and the river that he rediscovered were to be bitterly contested by European countries for more than two centuries. Soto's expedition obviously expanded greatly the geographical knowledge of the interior north of the Gulf of Mexico, and the compilation of detailed information on the Indian tribes and their civilization that came out of the expedition is highly significant in the study of Native American history.[3]

Colonization often follows exploration, but the Spaniards deferred immediate colonization within their eastern claim. Reasons advanced for the failure to colonize include a Spanish emphasis on protecting New Spain's northern frontier, an interest in South America, and the failure of Spanish explorers in the east to find wealth that could be easily taken from the Indians. Spain did not totally ignore the areas, however, as she sent Guido de Lavazares in 1558 to the Gulf where he reportedly landed on the Mississippi shore. Determining

that shallows and submerged lands in this region made it unfit for colonization, Lavazares decided to move eastward, where he discovered the Bay of
Filipina or Mobile Bay. In 1559, a large colonization party under the leadership
of Don Tristán de Luna y Arellano did colonize the areas of Mobile and
Pensacola, but after suffering extreme hardships the colony was removed in
1561. In yet another evidence of Spain's continuing interest in the east, Pedro
Menéndez de Avilés planted in 1565 the first permanent colony at St. Augustine
to blunt the intrusion of French Huguenots into the region.[4]

Although numerous Spanish excursions were made from the St. Augustine
base, French entry into the mid-continent and English settlement on the
Atlantic became important factors in the seventeenth century. From their
Canadian base, the French adopted an expansion policy westward and southward. Louis Joliet and Father Jacques Marquette provided an important leg in
the French expansion in their voyage down the Mississippi River in 1673 to the
vicinity of Rosedale, Mississippi. These two men embodied the major French
motives of furs and missions. The report of the Marquette-Joliet expedition
inspired René Robert Cavelier, Sieur de La Salle's 1682 descent of the Mississippi to its mouth, and his claiming and naming of the area "Louisiana" in
honor of his king. La Salle's initial success led to a second expedition in 1684.

La Salle maintained that France could establish a self-sufficient empire in
the New World by linking French holdings in Canada, the Louisiana area, and
Haiti by means of the Mississippi River. Such a proposal necessitated control
of the river by a colony at its mouth. Louis XIV supported this concept, and
La Salle's colonization party departed from France, but perhaps because of
faulty maps, the party missed the mouth of the river and landed in Texas.
During an attempt to walk to the mouth of the Mississippi, the party was beset
by hardships, dissension, and eventually the assassination of La Salle.

French intrusion into the Mississippi Valley evoked a response from Spain.
Officials in New Spain sent search parties by land and sea to ascertain the fate
of the La Salle expedition. Significantly, under Alonso de León, Damian
Massanet, and Francisco Hidalgo, the Spaniards placed missions, and later a
presidio, in Texas. In the southeast, Spain under the leadership of Andrés de
Arriola founded a post at Pensacola in November 1698.[5]

The Spanish fort in Pensacola was barely established when a French colonization party under Pierre Le Moyne, Sieur d'Iberville arrived with intentions to
settle Pensacola. Spanish officials politely but firmly advised the French to
move westward, where they built Fort Maurepas in 1699. From this Mississippi

FATHER MARQUETTE AND HIS SYMBOL OF PEACE.

Father Jacques Marquette and Louis Joliet, explorers for New France (Canada) of the Mississippi River in 1673. Courtesy of Historic New Orleans Collection.

Jean Baptiste Le Moyne, Sieur de Bienville, second governor of Louisiana. Courtesy of Mississippi Department of Archives and History.

base on Biloxi Bay the French expanded eastward to Mobile Bay by 1702, and westward to New Orleans by 1718, and from locations to the north ultimately spread into the entire Mississippi Valley.

The leadership of the French colony fell to Jean Baptiste Le Moyne, Sieur de Bienville, who for forty years was the dominant figure in Louisiana. The French in Louisiana were more commercial than agrarian in their pursuits; their indifference to the richness of the soil made the French colonies in the region a drain on rather than a contributor to the French treasury. Furthermore, French and Indian warfare depleted French resources that might otherwise have been productive in other projects. Some historians have noted that the paucity of laborers and unmarried women retarded French development. A final factor contributing to limited French success in the area was the incessant political bickering involving Bienville and other officials. Notable highlights of the French colonization included the construction of Fort Rosalie in 1716, the Indian massacre of the settlers of that fort in 1729, and the retaliatory destruction of the Natchez Indians by the French. Bienville's campaigns against the Chicka-saws were disastrous, although he did manage to sign a treaty with them. The French introduction of black slavery into Louisiana around 1719 did have a permanent impact. Additionally, the French should be credited for their explo-rations of Bay St. Louis and the Pearl River and establishment of Biloxi in 1719.[6]

Following the English settlements on the Atlantic and in the Caribbean, the stage was set for a series of wars involving Spain, France, and England in a contest for political supremacy. Although each war had a colonial phase, mini-mal colonial impact was reflected in the treaties ending the wars fought be-tween 1697 and 1748. However, the Treaty of Paris, 1763, which ended the Seven Years' War, produced monumental changes in the Mississippi Valley and Florida. France was ousted from in North America, and her former territory in the Mississippi Valley was divided between Spain and England. Except for the Isle of Orleans, England gained possession of all territory east of the Mississip-pi River including West Florida, and Spain was awarded the Isle of Orleans and territory to the west of the river. A 1764 commission defined the northern West Florida boundaries as 32° 28' of north latitude, the western boundary as the Mississippi and Iberville Rivers, and the eastern boundary as the Ap-alachicola and Chattahoochee Rivers. These boundaries encompassed approxi-mately one third of the present state of Mississippi.

When England took over West Florida, her officials envisioned the area as a potential economic plum in the emerging "New Colonial Policy." However, by 1764 the optimistic attitude was replaced by lamentation that the Spanish and French had failed to develop the area. George Johnstone, the first gover-nor of West Florida, devoted much of his attention to the eastern segment of the province, but his administration was beset by political dissension and failure to resolve the Indian conflicts. In 1767, Johnstone was recalled and for a short period replaced by his Lieutenant Governor, Montfort Browne.

Browne was among the first to acclaim the assets of the western section, specifically Natchez. He stated that the rich soil, abundant wild game, excel-lent river transportation, and good relations with the Indians made the area an excellent choice for settlement, and he recommended the establishment of towns at Natchez and Fort Bute. Browne, too, fell victim to political dissen-sion, and Elias Durnford, his replacement, continued to advocate moving more settlers into the Natchez area. Unfortunately, English officials in London early turned a deaf ear to his pleas and even withdrew the soldiers from Natchez and Fort Bute in 1767.

Fort of the Natchez, called Fort Rosalie, was constructed by forced Indian labor in 1716, destroyed by the Natchez Indians in 1729, and rebuilt from 1730–1734. Courtesy of Mississippi Department of Archives and History.

"Old Spanish Fort," located near Pascagoula, is actually an outbuilding for a French plantation of the 1720s. The structure is built of heavy timbers with spaces between filled with *bousillage*, a mixture of mud, moss, and shells, typical of the period. Courtesy of Historic Preservation Division of the Mississippi Department of Archives and History.

The appointment of Peter Chester as governor in 1770 was accompanied by significant change in the western province. Chester avowed that progress could be made only after Indian relations were improved. His conferences with the Indians and the reforms he instituted pretty well placated the Indians. The freedom from Indian conflicts permitted Chester to direct his attention to development of the western province. Endorsing the views of Browne, he maintained that the Natchez district offered greater potential and a healthier environment than the coastal region. Chester's policies obviously were effective as the volume of land patents increased in the 1770s. Most new arrivals to the region were from other English colonies, but German, Spanish, and French immigrants were also included. In the later 1770s, the immigrants to the region included a number of English Loyalists fleeing persecution during the American Revolution. Chester's administration offered liberal land grants, free transportation, military protection, and free rations as inducements to Protestant settlers who might come to the Natchez region. The success of his policies is evident in the population increase to more than 3,000 settlers in Natchez by 1774.

Although the achievements of Chester in the early 1770s were promising, the events of 1778 and 1779 were disastrous for his administration. James Willing, a former resident of Natchez, was commissioned by the Continental Congress to visit the Natchez settlers to obtain supplies and gain their loyalty for the Revolutionary cause. With his party of one hundred soldiers, Willing attacked and plundered the settlers in 1778. Bernardo de Gálvez, Governor of Spanish Louisiana, delivered the final blow to Chester's aspirations and English control when he recaptured West Florida in 1779.[7]

The events following the Revolutionary War are beyond the scope of this presentation; however, the United States replaced England as the adversary of Spain in the West Florida region. The boundary disputes, quarrels over navigational rights on the Mississippi, the Treaty of San Lorenzo, the purchase of Louisiana and the annexation of West Florida by the United States, and the Adams-Onis Treaty complete the final chapters in the international rivalry for hegemony in the region.

The European explorations, settlements, and international conflicts provide interesting narratives, but more significantly they permitted each of the participants to deposit a portion of their civilization in the area now the state of Mississippi. Obviously, the English heritage was dominant, as is evident in the enduring legacy of language, political concepts, religion, law, education, and

The Taylor-Nash house in Columbus (c. 1845) demonstrates the far-flung and long-lived influence of French architecture in the state. The raised cottage construction so typical of the French- and Spanish-settled areas of the Gulf Coast and Mississippi Valley features a brick lower story and wood frame second story, where the above-ground brick basement is less susceptible to moisture and the frame upper level remains cooler and open to breezes in the sub-tropical climate.

economics. Although Spain and France were limited in geographical area and sparsely populated, settlers from these countries significantly influenced Mississippi's heritage. In a broader context, Spanish and French settlers in the contiguous areas of present Mississippi brought much of their civilizations to be subsequently incorporated into Mississippi's history.

Spanish influences are reflected today in Mississippi's agriculture, livestock, architecture, law, and religion. Spain introduced cotton, rice, indigo, tobacco curing, sugar cane, wheat, barley, and citrus fruits to the region. Likewise, cattle, horses, swine, and goats are a legacy of the early Spanish settlers. A modern Mississippi cowboy rides his horse with lasso or lariat, bandanna, and other accoutrements as an inheritance from the early gaucho. Spanish architecture featuring the use of stucco, horseshoe arch, and tile may be observed throughout Mississippi. Since Spain was the first to grant land patents in the region, her grants were accepted by later authorities. Furthermore, her branding laws and property laws were in part incorporated into the codes of successive governments. Spain's introduction of Roman Catholicism might properly be noted in her contributions. Finally, Spain's role in the American Revolution was significant: not only did Spain recapture West Florida, but Gálvez's generous assistance to American agent Oliver Pollock and his support of the mission of George Rogers Clark significantly impacted the Revolutionary War.

France, too, has had a permanent influence in Mississippi. French family names and place names dot the southern portion of the state. French settlers also brought with them the Roman Catholicism which they practiced within their settlements. The introduction of black slaves and Bienville's "Black Code" of 1724 were later influential in the development of slavery in Mississippi. A lasting imprint can be found in Mississippi's French architecture which especially emphasizes the hip roof, casement windows, abundant use of dormers, and galleries.

In brief, the Mississippi heritage is enriched by the Indians and early European settlers. If Mississippi's culture cannot be described as a melting pot, it must be admitted that it has been profoundly influenced by the Indians, Spanish, and French who preceded the Anglo-Americans who came to dominate.

NOTES

1. For details of the Ponce de León and Pineda expeditions, see Woodbury Lowery, *The Spanish Settlements within the Present Limits of the United States, 1513–1561* (New York: G. P. Putnam's Sons, 1901; Russell & Russell, 1959), Chapters 1 and 2.

2. For accounts of his expedition, see Lowery, Chapter 3, and Cleve Hallenbeck, *Alvar Núñez, Cabeza de Vaca: The Journey and Route of the First European to Cross the Continent of North America, 1534–1536* (Glendale: Arthur H. Clark Co., 1940; Port Washington: Kennikat Press, 1971).

3. One account of the Soto expedition was written by a Portuguese, the Gentleman of Elvas, who accompanied the expedition. The author reportedly kept no

journal and subsequently wrote from memory. First published in 1557, the work is regarded by most authorities as the fullest account, but historians have questioned the accuracy of parts of his story. See Theodore H. Lewis, ed., *The Narratives of the Expedition of Hernando de Soto by the Gentleman of Elvas,* in J. Franklin Jameson, ed., *Original Narratives of Early American History* (New York: Charles Scribner's Sons, 1907; Barnes & Noble, 1946), 127–272.

4. Lowery, 351–377.

5. John F. Bannon, "The Spaniards in the Mississippi Valley," in John Francis McDermott, ed., *The Spanish in the Mississippi Valley, 1726–1804* (Urbana: University of Illinois Press, 1974), 3–15.

6. Walter G. Howell, "The French Period, 1699–1763," in Richard A. McLemore, ed., *A History of Mississippi* (Hattiesburg: University & College Press of Mississippi, 1973), 1:110–133.

7. Byrle A. Kynerd, "British West Florida," in McLemore, 1:134–157.

SUGGESTED READINGS

Bolton, Herbert Eugene. *The Spanish Borderlands: A Chronicle of Old Florida and the Southwest.* The Chronicles of America Series, ed. Allen Johnson, vol. 23. New Haven: Yale University Press, 1921.

Caughey, John W. *Bernardo de Gálvez in Louisiana, 1776–1783.* Berkeley: University of California Press, 1934.

Crouse, Nellis M. *Lemoyne d'Iberville, Soldier of New France.* Ithaca: Cornell University Press, 1954.

Giraud, Marcel. *A History of French Louisiana.* Baton Rouge: Louisiana State University Press, 1974.

Haynes, Robert V. *The Natchez District and the American Revolution.* Jackson: University Press of Mississippi, 1976.

Johnson, Cecil. *British West Florida, 1763–1783.* New Haven: Yale University Press, 1943.

McDermott, John F., ed. *The Spanish in the Mississippi Valley, 1762–1804.* Urbana: University of Illinois Press, 1974.

McLemore, Richard A., ed. *A History of Mississippi.* Hattiesburg: University and College Press of Mississippi, 1973.

Wright, J. Leitch. *Anglo-Spanish Rivalry in North America.* Athens: University of Georgia Press, 1971.

Africans in Colonial
and Territorial Mississippi

Robert L. Jenkins

For nearly a century, part of today's Mississippi was an important center of European colonial activity. France, which established the first permanent white settlement on Mississippi soil in 1699, controlled the area as part of its sprawling Louisiana colony. The French were supplanted by the British in 1763, who in turn were succeeded by the Spanish, both of whom included the Mississippi region in their West Florida colony. For all of these powers, the Natchez country became the centerpiece of their Mississippi interest. None of these European countries realized their ambitions in Mississippi, but each in its own way influenced the area's historical development. The foundations which they laid were especially beneficial to the energetic, land-hungry Americans who came into the region at the end of the eighteenth century. Territorial Mississippi under American control almost immediately began to yield the kinds of economic successes that had long eluded the colonial powers.

The story of Mississippi's colonial and territorial experience, however, goes beyond the activities of Europeans and early American white settlers. Central is the role that thousands of Africans and their American-born descendants played in shaping the early history and economic development of the region.

Ironically, this role even manifested itself in the ingenious work of a Mississippi slave, whose efforts in helping to perfect the cotton gin influenced the transformation of the region's economy and thereby enlarged and tightened the yoke of bondage around his people. Like their white counterparts, however, most of these people were ordinary folk; they worked, played, interacted with non-Africans, shared dreams, sometimes drank heavily, and even resisted oppression. In this respect, they all contributed to the diversity of the region.

To be sure, the Africans' contributions to Mississippi during these eras were not always made willingly, but that fact neither detracts from their value nor lessens their importance. Clearly, the continuous and rapid growth of the black population and Mississippi's unusual reliance on their labor during both the colonial (1699–1798) and territorial (1798–1817) periods attest to the significance of blacks in the area's advancement. In many ways, their presence impacted on the character of Mississippi society and influenced its way of life for generations thereafter, as it continues to affect the state today.

These results, however, were hardly predictable when France first settled the region. France was determined to build a profitable agricultural economy in the Lower Mississippi Valley, but apparently the plan did not initially involve the use of African slaves. From the outset, however, Louisiana officials experienced problems with their Canadian and French subjects' neglect of farming. Indeed, lack of interest and inability of the settlers to engage in even simple subsistence agriculture caused Jean Baptiste LeMoyne, Sieur de Bienville, Louisiana's second and most outstanding governor, to lament the prospects for the colony's success. The failure of Louisiana to attract a sizeable number of immigrants, particularly experienced farmers and female colonists, exacerbated its early problems and forced Bienville to seek relief from Paris with proposals for the importation of Africans.[1]

Little came of Bienville's requests. Inadequate colonial financial resources and France's war commitments precluded any immediate opportunity for home authorities to address the matter of African laborers favorably.[2] Instead, Louisiana attempted to meet its labor demands with Indian slavery and white indentured servitude. These efforts proved as unsatisfactory as they had been in European colonies elsewhere. Louisiana colonists became disenchanted with both the dependability and the quality of forced Indian labor. Hence, as a matter of policy, Indian enslavement, except in cases of punishment, was abandoned. White indentures were considered little better, primarily because of their difficulty in adapting to Louisiana's climate. According to one colonial official, whites simply found it "impossible . . . to do work in the fields, especially in the summer."[3]

The consequences of Louisiana's problems became evident to other observers as well. In their determination to escape the rigors of physical labor, the colonists themselves became so desperate for African workers that many of them threatened to return to France unless slaves were imported. As one historian of the early colony has written, Paris officials soon realized that "the inhabitant working on his own, without the help of the black was doomed to failure." Because of a languishing economy and a newly reorganized colonial plan, France increasingly turned to black labor for its colony's survival in the third decade of its ownership.[4]

Africans first appeared in the province in significant numbers after 1719. Their arrival was largely the result of the work of financier John Law and his Company of the Indies. Law's company, which acquired long-term operating rights to Louisiana in 1717, obligated itself to import 3,000 slaves into the colony before the expiration of its charter. In 1721 alone, the company sent 1,312 Africans to Louisiana. Virtually every year thereafter shiploads of Africans arrived in the colony from the Guinea coast or the West Indies; by 1760, near the end of the French period of Louisiana, there were 6,000 slaves laboring in the colony. Most of these Africans were located in the New Orleans and Mobile regions, but others were distributed in small numbers throughout the remaining lower districts of the colony. The Natchez region, which was first occupied by the French in 1716 following the construction of Fort Rosalie, was the most important "Upper Mississippi" settlement; by 1723 it was populated by more than 300 settlers, including 111 Africans.[5]

Law's company never realized the gains it anticipated from Louisiana, and it surrendered its colonial charter far ahead of the expiration date. Nevertheless, the company did much to advance the province in the thirteen years of its control. During the decade of the 1720s, for example, it stimulated considerable interest in the fertile Natchez sector. Officials predicted great economic success for the area, provided settlers were "assisted by negroes." Appealing descriptions of "the good quality of the land and the ease of clearing it" were especially attractive to Caribbean planters who learned that the country could sustain both tobacco and indigo cultures. Natchez planters placed the greatest emphasis on tobacco production, although its quality did not compare favorably with that produced in other colonial areas. A number of Frenchmen acquired large concessions in the region and extensively employed slaves to

John Law, a Scottish financier, was responsible for
importing large numbers of
African slaves into Loui-
siana. Courtesy of Mis-
sissippi Department of
Archives and History.

cultivate crops of wheat, rice, and cotton in addition to tobacco and indigo.
Slaves also did important work in producing silk and a variety of "dressed
timber," pitch, and tar for colonial export.[6]

Skilled work also consumed the attention of the colony's slaves. As appren-
tices to some of the settlers, many of these workers learned valuable trades as
masons, carpenters, tailors, and caulkers. But it was the most demanding and
strenuous of the necessary labor that Africans were generally expected to
perform. Besides plantation work, their duties included virtually everything
from constructing and improving the roads and levees to serving in the transport business, handling goods and other related jobs on ship and land. Women
worked in traditional domestic areas, but they also labored alongside the men
performing back-breaking and tedious work, loading and unloading boats and
pulling weeds from the grounds surrounding the "king's warehouses" and
other buildings.[7]

The period when Natchez planters would oversee massive estates manned by dozens of slaves lay far in the future, but even at this early time in the region's history there were portents of that era. By the end of the 1720, two men, a Mr. LeBlanc and a Mr. Kolly, had already acquired more than twenty slaves each. Sixty slaves cultivated the tobacco and wheat crops on the six hundred arpents plantation owned by March Anthony Hubert de St. Malo. By 1727 there were 280 Africans in the Natchez country, this number representing 39.2 percent of the settlement's total population. Such figures made an impact on Louisiana's labor shortfall, but hardly eliminated it. Between 1723 and 1731, an average of 350 Africans were imported annually into Louisiana, but their uneven distribution throughout the colony and West Indian competition for their labor limited agricultural expansion everywhere in the country. Hence, the demand for African laborers remained high. Such was the case among planters wanting to expand their operations and also among small landholders, who often desired only a single slave to relieve themselves of some of the drudgery and toil of farming on the Mississippi frontier.[8]

Slaves were a valuable commodity in Louisiana, and their costs reflected this fact. Initially they sold for an average of 600 livres, about the same as most Indian slaves. In less than four years after Law's company initiated the trade, however, the average cost had risen more than sixty-six percent. As was the case elsewhere in New World colonies, slave prices in Louisiana varied, influenced by such factors as sex, age, health, and individual skills. Understandably, "exceptional" slaves were the most expensive. Highly skilled males, for example, frequently sold for as much as 1,200 livres, and an exceptional female "Piece d' Indies" could command a price of 2,000 livres. The Company of the Indies attempted to make it relatively easy for Louisianians to purchase slaves through a liberal repayment policy, but except for large landholders in productive areas such as Natchez, apparently few small independent farmers could realistically afford the costs.[9]

The increasing number of Louisiana blacks and Bienville's expectations about their role in the colony led to the region's first slave laws. Drafted in 1724 by Bienville, the *Code Noir* was a comprehensive edict regulating the activities and responsibilities of slaves and masters alike. Included in the document were controls and restrictions similarly applicable to slaves elsewhere in the Western Hemisphere. Circumscribed, for example, were the slaves' opportunities to marry, to engage in personal commercial ventures, to accumulate property, to carry firearms, to assemble at night, and to leave their places of residence. Under pain of severe punishment, even death, slaves were not allowed to

LE CODE NOIR

OU

EDIT DU ROY,

SERVANT DE REGLEMENT

POUR

*Le Gouvernement & l'Adminiftration de la Juftice, Police,
Difcipline & le Commerce des Efclaves Negres, dans
la Province & Colonie de la Loüifianne.*

Donné à Verfailles au mois de Mars 1724.

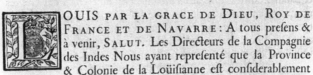

OUIS PAR LA GRACE DE DIEU, ROY DE
FRANCE ET DE NAVARRE: A tous prefens &
à venir, SALUT. Les Directeurs de la Compagnie
des Indes Nous ayant reprefenté que la Province
& Colonie de la Loüifianne eft confiderablement
eftablie par un grand nombre de nos Sujets, lefquels fe fervent
d'Efclaves Negres pour la culture des terres; Nous avons jugé
qu'il eftoit de noftre authorité & de noftre Juftice, pour la
confervation de cette Colonie, d'y eftablir une loy & des regles
certaines, pour y maintenir la difcipline de l'Eglife Catholique,

j

Title page of the *Code Noir*, drafted by Governor Bienville in 1724 as the region's first slave laws. Courtesy of The Historic New Orleans Collection.

commit "thefts of importance" and were forbidden to strike any white person. For habitual runaways, the governor's code prescribed ear cropping, branding, hamstringing, or execution. Masters who refused to provide for their bondsmen in health as well as sickness and old age subjected themselves to fines, and owners were not permitted to mutilate or otherwise inhumanely mistreat their slaves. By law, slaveholders were required to provide slaves religious instruction, and, at death, a Catholic burial. Finally, masters jeopardized their slaves to confiscation if they worked them on Sundays and Catholic holy days.[10]

Despite some notably harsh provisions in Bienville's code, it was otherwise unique for its liberality. It sought, for example, to make valuable and productive naturalized inhabitants of emancipated slaves by granting them the same rights and privileges held by other Frenchmen. One provision voided sales when they separated wives and husbands belonging to the same master, and another forbade the sale of children under age fourteen away from their parents.[11] By nullifying such sales, Louisiana, if not in practice then at least legally, refused to sanction the complete breakup of slave families, one of the most cruel and reprehensible practices associated with the institution everywhere it existed. Mississippi's practices in later years would depart considerably from the humane considerations embodied in this region's first set of slave laws.

Clearly, African slaves were playing a decisive role in the evolution and growth of the Natchez country. However, the destructive Natchez Indian War halted this process. The Indians attacked and destroyed Fort Rosalie in late 1729, kidnapping or setting free the slaves and killing or driving away most of the white settlers. The settlement's 200,000-pound tobacco harvest awaiting shipment to France was also destroyed. French retribution for the massacre around Natchez was complete; these Indians as a separate independent tribe in Mississippi ceased to exist. But with the destruction of Fort Rosalie, French interest in developing the Natchez district economically all but ended. Its population murdered or dispersed, the deserted settlement thereafter consisted of only a small garrison of soldiers. Apparently, neither French nor African newcomers sought the area in the remaining thirty-four years of France's control of Louisiana.[12]

England's defeat of France in 1763 in the Seven Years' War ended French colonialism in North America. With that victory, England became the new owner of Mississippi, administering the region as part of its colony of West Florida. British rule over Mississippi was of short duration, lasting only until the latter years of the American Revolution. During this period, however, the English made a concerted effort to develop the Mississippi country, particularly in diverting population to the region. Fully aware of its economic potential, the British made Natchez the greatest beneficiary of this renewed interest. Under England's control the district expanded to include most of southwestern Mississippi, and extended as far north as the mouth of the Yazoo River near present-day Vicksburg. Immigrants, black and white, came to the area and its population grew steadily, albeit slowly.

When the British initially occupied West Florida, however, they found a sparsely populated area, particularly in the western reaches of the province. From the outset, authorities realized that attracting a stable population to the region was vital to its progress, and a liberal land-grant policy was implemented to achieve this end. At the discretion of colonial officials, exceptionally large grants were made to prominent Britons and war veterans, but a formal policy embodying less favoritism proved more effective. Under the system, each head of a family who moved to West Florida was eligible for one hundred acres of land and fifty additional acres for each dependent in the household, including servants and slaves. For the small sum of five shillings per fifty acres, the recipient of this "family right" could purchase up to 1,000 additional acres.[13] The policy was an attractive inducement to settlers seeking economic opportunities, but it also revealed an understanding that the future of the colony did not rest entirely with white settlers. Authorities had few illusions about the role Africans were to play in the colony. Clearly, as its first governor George Johnstone wrote, West Florida's success would ultimately depend on African "slave[s], without which it will be impossible to raise the colony to any eminence."[14]

Johnstone's argument was the same one that the French had used in their appeal for African laborers. But it was a subject that English officials had already learned well from their nearby Georgia experience. Slavery was originally outlawed in this frontier colony, but the economy had languished until African labor was widely accepted seventeen years after its founding. The mistakes of Georgia were not to be repeated in the frontier environs of West Florida.

Perhaps nowhere were Africans' roles expected to be more crucial than in the rich alluvial soil along the eastern banks of the Mississippi. The Mississippi Gulf Coast, as it had been under the French, remained largely inconsequential; only a few families inhabited the infertile Biloxi region. Some settlers resided in the Pascagoula and Pearl River country, but generally these locations, too, garnered little newcomer interest.[15] French planters had already proved the Natchez soil capable of yielding abundant tobacco crops. Understandably, then, immigrants, primarily from other English colonies, found the Natchez country especially appealing. Many of them were already familiar with tobacco production and wasted little time in turning their black laborers to the cultivation of this plant.

Most of these colonists brought their slaves with them when they moved to the area. Others acquired them directly through the African trade or purchased available slaves from traders in the British West Indies and North American colonies. Whatever the origin of the slaves, their appearance and growth in the province did much to influence the character, progress, and complexion of the Mississippi country. In 1772, Governor Elias Durnford reported only a few settlers residing in the district, but they owned "considerable property in slaves." Although still very much a frontier outpost, the area grew materially during the next two years; approximately 2,500 whites had migrated there, and they employed more than 600 slaves.[16]

The black presence became more notable during the American Revolution as numbers continued to escalate. During the period, persecuted Tories from the older English colonies sought and received official asylum in the safety of the loyalist Natchez region. Although most of these newcomers were small slaveholders, owning fewer than ten Africans before their resettlement in Natchez, many others were more affluent and brought numerous slaves with them. In 1777, for example, South Carolinians William Marshall, Jr., and David Holmes emigrated with twenty and twenty-two slaves respectively. Another South Carolina loyalist, John Turner, led a party of approximately forty whites to the Natchez region in 1778; they were accompanied by 500 slaves. Exactly how many blacks arrived in the region during this era cannot be accurately determined, but apparently the number was substantial. According to one authority, by 1779, near the end of the English period, Natchez's population had nearly doubled from its 1774 estimate of 3,100. Africans probably comprised the greatest percentage of this increase, coming directly into the region as they did with their masters and as regular consignments of the slave trade. These Africans, along with the hundreds of others that preceded them to the western province area, devoted their time to raising a variety of vegetable and fruit crops on the smaller farms and to the production of tobacco, indigo, and small quantities of cotton on the larger plantations. Export products of raw

Drawing depicting plantation slaves at work. Courtesy of Mississippi Department of Archives and History.

timber, lumber, and barrel staves brought significant additional revenue into the region for some residents and consumed considerable labor time from the African workers.[17]

As both laborers and objects of exchange, African slaves in West Florida were a great source of wealth. Naturally, their monetary worth varied and fluctuated as it did in other colonial ventures, but at no time was their value insignificant. Their market prices verify this. Throughout the era, male slaves sold for an average of between 250 and 300 Spanish dollars; female slaves averaged about fifty dollars less. Generally, sellers had the advantage in the more lucrative Mississippi market. For a healthy slave in 1776, the last good trading year for that marketplace, Africans sold for an average of fifty pounds ($215). But West Florida buyers often paid more handsomely for some purchases. William Ogelvie's expenditure of 500 Spanish-milled dollars for Tonette, "a mulatto wench," was the highest price paid for a slave during the English era.[18] Ogelvie's reason for paying so much for this "mulatto wench" is unknown, but apparently he was not troubled by her high purchase price.

Professionals were not the only ones who profited from the buying and selling of slaves in West Florida. African servants represented a good investment for individual owners, who frequently merchandised them in single or small lots. Perhaps no one was more successful at this than William Dunbar, a large slaveholder and wealthy planter who lived above Manchac on the eastern side of the Mississippi during the British period. Dunbar frequently bought and sold slaves for simple investment purposes. On one occasion he sold five males for 1,300 Spanish dollars, an average of 260 dollars each. Shortly thereafter he received 220 Spanish dollars for a female slave. How much of these sums represented clear profit is unknown, but he apparently found the transactions lucrative. Moreover, he seemed to have little compunction about the immorality of the business. Even while he lamented the death of his favorite slave Cato, "the most likely negro on the plantation," he could not help but express his grief in financial terms; Cato, he declared, "wou'd have fetched at Market a hundred pounds sterling."[19]

That the English considered these slaves valuable is undeniable. Bernard Romans, a former colonial officer in West Florida and its first historian, declared that "a Negroe at the Mississippi is reckoned to bring in [to] his master a hundred dollars per annum, besides his share towards all the provisions consumed in the family."[20] Small wonder, then, that some Natchez residents, even in this era of frontier rawness, could afford to purchase numerous luxury items, including fine clothing and expensive wines and liquors.[21]

Romans insinuated that because of their value, Africans in the Mississippi country were treated better than slaves in Carolina.[22] West Florida's provincial laws for governing its slaves, however, did not provide a mild system of servitude. Indeed, in many ways, as it appears in law, West Florida slavery was harsh and clearly reflected the economic value colonists associated with the institution.

The West Florida measure differed little from other codes in prohibiting or restricting slave alcohol consumption, assembly, carrying of firearms, and absence from plantations without written permission. Slaves were also expressly forbidden to engage in private commercial activities. The theft of a slave was punishable by death, a penalty that says much about the importance West Floridians attached to the institution of slavery. Expectedly, slaves convicted of

William Dunbar, a prosperous slaveholder and planter whose fortune was built in part on slave trade. Photograph courtesy of Mississippi Department of Archives and History.

arson or of deliberately inflicting injury on a white person suffered capital punishment. The code was particularly severe in its penalties for generally inconsequential infractions. Runaways, for example, were subjected to lashings and public humiliation; for the offense of setting adrift a canoe, the prescribed punishment was execution.[23] Historian Robin Fabel's evaluation of this code certainly seems incontestable. The statute, he writes, "sought to create and perpetuate an inflexible system in which all those who were not white—color was the 'badge of servitude,' read the act—had an important but restricted and subordinate place in society."[24] How much of West Florida's slave code was stringently applied is open to conjecture, but the African's lowly position as an inferior remained basically unchanged for nearly twenty years of British rule in West Florida. That status certainly did not improve when Spain replaced England in the last two decades of the eighteenth century.

Under British control African slavery became a permanent fixture in the Natchez country. Both the institution and the settlement, however, lasted far longer than did the British as colonizers of West Florida. Like the French, the British experienced violent confrontations which directly influenced their exit from the region. Spain's entry into the American Revolutionary War in 1779 posed a direct danger to largely unprotected British West Florida. In control of New Orleans and Louisiana west of the Mississippi since the end of the Seven Years' War, Spain's presence in the river region made the loyalist Natchez country particularly vulnerable. In less than a year after Spain entered the conflict, a formidable force under the leadership of Don Bernardo de Gálvez, the Governor-General of Louisiana, had successfully seized the major British fortifications on the Mississippi. By the end of 1781, the entire Gulf region of East and West Florida had become a Spanish lake.[25]

Spain's occupancy of West Florida in the post-Revolutionary War era continued an already vibrant interest in the Mississippi region. In increasing numbers during the period, Americans took advantage of Spain's offer of liberal land grants and joined an already predominantly English population to further develop the Natchez District. In 1784, the district's population totaled 1,619 persons; by the end of the Spanish era sixteen years later some 5,318 persons resided in the region. Slaves comprised important components of this increase. Spanish officials encouraged the growth of the African population by providing additional land to immigrants who brought slaves with them. Between 1785 and 1796 their total increased 134 percent; by the latter date the 2,110 estimated Africans district-wide represented forty percent of the area's total population.[26]

The slave increase was the direct result of Spain's economic initiatives in the district. During the 1780s, officials devoted much of their energy to finding a viable cash crop. Because of Natchez's experience with tobacco production, authorities naturally encouraged the development of this product. Planters in the province expanded their operations, benefiting from Spain's guaranteed tobacco market and the hard cash the government provided them in crop subsidies. In 1789, tobacco growers in the district had a bumper crop, producing more than 1.4 million pounds of the weed. This tobacco prosperity, however, did not last. In 1790, economic problems in Spain and poor export markets interacted to eliminate Natchez tobacco production. Emphasis was then placed on indigo, which thrived in the district for several years, although only a few large planters grew it abundantly. Soil exhaustion, along with market and insect problems, soon affected its cultivation, however, and by 1795 it too had all but disappeared from the Natchez country.[27]

Naturally slaves played a critical role in both these crop cultures. They planted, cultivated, and harvested tobacco and indigo crops and were involved in their storage, processing, and transportation. In all aspects of preparation of these crops, planters naturally used slave labor, though there were several disadvantages to this system. Processing the dye from the indigo plant, for example, caused considerable health problems for the slaves.[28] Most slaveholders were genuinely concerned about slave health matters, if for no other reason than their effects on property values. Hence, many planters were probably not especially saddened to see the disappearance of the area's indigo culture.

Because there were not many industries in colonial Mississippi, slaves performed few tasks in these areas. Providing cypress logs for the naval stores industry, however, was one of their most conspicuous non-agricultural activities. During the fall months, they labored in the district's swamps cutting logs, which were then skillfully arranged in raft-like patterns and floated down the river to New Orleans.[29] Obviously, this was exacting work and differed little from the arduous labor with which most slaves in colonial and territorial Mississippi were most associated.

Near the end of the Spanish period, black labor was increasingly identified with cotton. The rapid emergence of cotton as a major cash crop in colonial Mississippi certainly made the loss of both tobacco and indigo more acceptable. This crop's rise in importance occurred because of a significant technological breakthrough. Eli Whitney's invention of the cotton gin in 1793 revolutionized the process of separating the seed from the lint and thereby provided Mississippi and the South the staple crop they had long sought.

News of Whitney's invention spread rapidly. Despite his patent, descriptions of the gin soon resulted in the appearance of various adaptations and imitations across the South. In the summer of 1795, colonial Mississippi saw its own version of the machine. After hearing about Whitney's gin, Daniel Clark, a prominent Natchez district planter, examined a traveler's sketch of the invention and immediately employed three men on his plantation to replicate it. Barclay, one of Clark's skilled slave mechanics, was a key member of this manufacturing team. With nothing but Clark's imperfect second-hand description and a crude drawing, Barclay and the other men completed an improved version of the gin that served as the standard for subsequent models in Mississippi.[30]

By reducing and simplifying the processing time and, subsequently, the

cost, the gin made cotton production a truly profitable enterprise. Consequently, turning to its cultivation on a large scale was not a decision that
Mississippi planters hesitated in making. All of the necessary ingredients
seemed to be in place. Besides the gin, and of course the land itself, no other
resource was more central to their decision than the readily available labor
supply. Experience had already demonstrated cotton to be a crop amenable to
slave labor; the gin simply helped to solidify the relationship. For cotton to
render the financial gains most clearly anticipated, however, Africans would be
required to play a role greater than ever before in the region's economic life.
Within a generation, both terms, "cotton" and "slaves," would virtually become synonymous with Mississippi's name; ironically, Barclay's ingenuity
helped to accomplish that.

After years of controversy over ownership of the "Yazoo Strip," Spain in 1798
finally surrendered to the United States its control of Mississippi north of the
thirty-first degree of north latitude. By then the Natchez region was already
prospering from cotton and slaves. Planter William Dunbar, now a prominent
resident of the district, could easily declare in 1799 that cotton was "by far the
most profitable crop we have ever undertaken in this country." Slaves on
Dunbar's plantation had already made him one of territorial Mississippi's largest cotton producers; in 1800 he exported more than 100 bales of the fiber to
Liverpool. African slaves were becoming so valuable in the emerging cotton
economy, Dunbar claimed, that a male of "established character" could command a maximum selling price of $600, while "a fellow not known" normally
went for $500. Demands in the territory, he wrote, were high, as the region
clamored for "more slaves."[31]

And "more slaves" came. Between 1800 and 1820, their heavy importation
swelled the black population of both old and new regions of territorial Mississippi, although never completely meeting the avid demands of southwestern
planters. In 1800 there were 2,995 slaves residing in the two counties comprising the old Natchez district. By 1810, the total number of blacks in all of the
territory that is now Mississippi had escalated to 14,706, though most of them
still inhabited the country around the Mississippi River. In 1820, about two
years after Mississippi's admission to the Union, the slave population had more
than doubled, totaling 32,814 persons.[32]

In the years between the beginning and the end of Mississippi's territorial
status, these slaves came primarily from the border states and the upper South.
Victims of the profitable but notorious internal slave trade, some of them

Negroes For Sale at
AUCTION.

On *THURSDAY*, the 10th of the present Month, at the Store of Messrs. *H. Postlethwaite & Co.* in Natchez, will be sold at Public Auction, all the SLAVES belonging to the estate of the late *Col. John Steele,* being 29 in number, consisting of 6 Men, 7 Women, 4 Boys from 8 to 14 years of age, 2 Girls from 10 to 12 years of age, and 10 Children under 10 years of age.....Three of those men have Families among the above Slaves.

Terms.....One half payable 1st of April next, and one half in 12 months, secured by notes with approved endorsers, payable at Bank.....To those who may purchase one or more Families, better terms will be given.

The Slaves can be seen at the late place of residence of the deceasad, at any time previous to the sale.

Handbill advertising a slave auction in Natchez, Mississippi. Courtesy of Mississippi Department of Archives and History.

Illustration from *Africans in the New World, 1493–1834,* by Larissa V. Brown (Providence, 1988). Courtesy of John Carter Brown Library, Providence, Rhode Island.

reached the territory via the Gulf of Mexico or the Mississippi, but thousands of others, particularly during the early territorial period, arrived in the region overland, along the Natchez Trace. Primarily used to deliver the mail between Nashville and Natchez, the Trace was frequently a beehive of activity as long lines of slave coffles originating in Virginia, South Carolina, or Tennessee moved to the old Southwest and were sold in the lucrative markets of Vicksburg, Natchez, and New Orleans.[33]

Whether the slave was an old or recent arrival in the territory, he/she found cultivating cotton on the Mississippi frontier a difficult experience. If it was virgin land, it had first to be cleared, and that was no easy task in the Mississippi climate. Days were usually long, the toil laborious. Little changed for slaves even after the land was cultivated. On the large plantations manned by dozens of laborers, the hands went to the fields at first day and worked in gangs, hoeing, plowing, and eventually picking the cotton. At critical junctures in the cycle, even Sundays were not sacrosanct, especially at harvest, the most demanding period of the seasons. Dragging a heavy cotton bag in Mississippi's heat and humidity and having to stoop constantly or bend to extract the cotton from the boll was a tiring exercise, and it took a toll on even the most physically fit. Malingering brought outright punishment, or certainly a threat of it. Depending on the time of year, other tasks might also necessitate gang-organized work. There might, for example, be a need for a cotton-ginning gang, a fence-building gang, or a corn-pulling gang. Women were not generally excluded from such activities; if exemptions occurred, they were in particularly dangerous or extremely heavy physical work such as digging ditches, felling trees, or rolling logs. When slaves understandably appeared sluggish in conducting their field work, it often had more to do with lack of vitality than with being lazy or irresponsible, as some slaveholders believed.[34]

Clearly this was a smothering work environment for the slaves. Of course, not all Mississippi slaves were involved in cultivating cotton. Indeed, large numbers of them during the territorial period were not agricultural workers at all. Because territorial Mississippi's population was larger than that of colonial Mississippi and hence its services and needs were greater, Africans performed in a wider variety of jobs. Besides common laborers and the numerous classes of domestics, in the various towns and villages lived slaves who labored as mechanics, draymen, and hostlers. Black tradesmen skilled as ginwrights and wheelwrights, brickmasons, blacksmiths, carpenters, and other building craftsmen were often hired out by their masters to the chagrin of many similarly skilled whites of the community. If permitted to hire their own time, as many skilled blacks did in violation of the territory's slave code, hirelings generally found a greater opportunity to enjoy various privileges and freedom of movement not available to most slaves.[35]

Some Africans depended on these and other skills as free persons of color during the era. Never a large numerical class in Mississippi before the Civil War, free blacks totaled only 182 persons in 1800. By 1820 the number had risen to 458, only to peak twenty years later at the paltry total of 1,366. Living primarily in "urban centers" like Natchez, where economic opportunities generally tended to be better, most of these people were of mixed African and European parentage. Whites relegated the small percentage of darker skinned "true blacks" to the lowest tier of the free black class, but neither the mulatto nor "true black" free person of color found life in Mississippi particularly favorable. Mississippi law presumed the free black "*prima facie* to be a slave," and society treated him or her little better. Only the right to own property distinguished free blacks substantially from bonded blacks; otherwise they suffered from limitations and discrimination in virtually all aspects of Mississippi life. Although not the pariahs in the territorial period that Mississippi whites would later perceive them to be, even in this era, regardless of their character, they were distrusted—feared and carefully watched as potential instigators of violent slave resistance.[36] Yet throughout the period they endured and added in their own small way to the evolution and progress of Mississippi from one level of development to the next.

Perhaps in ways more evident than in any other slave state, free blacks in the Mississippi country were true anomalies. Early codes governing Africans certainly did not speak to the contrary.[37] But understandably, it was slaves whom the codes addressed most directly, and they left little doubt as to where and how these people were to fit into Mississippi society. In a period when the African population was already showing signs of becoming the largest group in the territory, whites intended the law to secure themselves in their rights to slave property and in their persons as well.

These laws were stringent. Typically, a litany of restrictions was placed on the slaves' mobility, their involvement in buying and selling, the keeping of firearms and ammunition, the making of seditious speeches, and unlawful assembly. Any time more than five slaves gathered, a white man was required to be in attendance. Even in church services, plantation slave preachers were forbidden to exhort unless two reputable whites were present, and nonresident

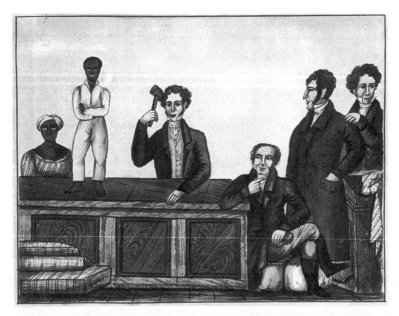

Illustration depicting a slave auction. Courtesy of The Historic New Orleans
Collection.

blacks other than these preachers were excluded from the worship. Slaves could
not consume liquor or speak "abusive and provoking" language to any white
person. Punishment ranging from ten but "not exceeding thirty-nine lashes"
administered "on his or her back, well laid on" was frequently the sentence an
offending slave could expect from justices of the peace for misdemeanor infractions.

Slaves were made to understand that whites would not tolerate serious
threats to their hegemony. The law was explicit in prescribing severe penalties
for crimes committed against white persons and their property. Any black,
slave or free, suffered death if convicted of plotting servile insurrection, attempted murder, attempted rape, assault and battery, the maiming of any
white person, or arson. The law decreed that blacks found guilty of certain
felonies not punishable by death were to be burned in the hand and administered "other corporal punishment." A second felony judgment subjected the
convicted to execution.

The laws embodied little real recognition of the slaves' humanity. Although
the 1817 constitution ending Mississippi's territorial status obligated masters to

treat their slaves "with humanity" and to "abstain from all injuries to them extending to life or limb,"[38] it did little to establish a positive environment to elevate the human spirit. By statute, slaves were expressly forbidden to own livestock of any kind and were excluded from any right to "cultivate cotton for their own use." [39] A later provision denied them opportunity to become literate.[40] The slave code may seldom have been strictly or consistently enforced in early Mississippi, as one historian has argued,[41] but on those occasions when it was employed, it must have intensified the oppression most blacks already felt in the territory. Studied comparatively, it certainly contained no provisions reminiscent of the liberal spirit embodied in parts of Bienville's earlier *Code Noir*.

Oppression was certainly not peculiar to Africans of the territorial period. By its very nature, human slavery was inherently oppressive, and Africans surely felt it throughout their Mississippi provincial and territorial experiences. Perhaps it was largely for this reason that slaves occasionally sought release through violence. Sometimes these outbursts simply manifested themselves in striking whites in defiance of the law. Obviously, these were viewed as serious infractions, as in the case of the "violent assaults upon the overseers of Mr. Lintots and Mr. Moores slaves" in November, 1800. Leaders often regarded a rash of such slave behavior as the prelude to more widespread violence against whites. The governor of Mississippi certainly did in this case.[42]

There was just cause to be concerned over slave rebellions. Indeed, the likelihood of such uprisings had been a part of the institution from its earliest beginnings in the region. In the summer of 1730, a slave named Samba headed a conspiracy of several persons near New Orleans to kill the whites residing along the river and "to make themselves free possessors of the country."[43] The plot was revealed by a female slave who, after being struck by a soldier for disobeying an order, blurted in anger that "the French should not long insult negroes!" Eight of the leading suspects were duly arrested and severely tortured until they admitted guilt. All eight of the conspirators, including Samba, were eventually "condemned to be broke alive on the wheel"; the woman was hanged.[44]

No uprising was more serious in colonial Mississippi than the massacre which the Natchez Indians perpetrated against the settlers at Fort Rosalie. These Indians, who felt terribly victimized by the white presence in their country, conspired with other nearby disaffected tribes to expel the French from the region. Apparently it was relatively easy to interest some area blacks as well. With promises of freedom and a share of the booty, a number of slaves in the vicinity of the fort were persuaded by the Indians to aid them in the attack.[45] Naturally French authorities, bent on retribution, hunted down these black conspirators as relentlessly as they hunted the Natchez.

Alliances comprised of black and red men were the kind that the French had certainly hoped to avoid. Such coalitions posed a direct threat to French survival in the region. In their effort to keep blacks and reds apart, the French effected a strategy based on the concept of "divide and conquer." Often they successfully implemented this policy by pitting Africans against the Indians in military campaigns. Such a confrontation occurred shortly after French retaliation against the Natchez Indians in 1730. Authorities, feigning suspicion of a joint slave and Indian insurrection, armed the slaves and ordered them to attack the small Chouacha tribe residing near New Orleans. Governor Etienne Périer's only purpose for this action was to create antagonism between the two races; it worked. The black mercenaries came close to annihilating the tribe.[46] More important to French design, however, was the fact that the conflict successfully "rendered the Indians [in Louisiana] mortal enemies of the negroes."[47]

Concern over potentially destructive slave uprisings did not escape the British in the Mississippi region. In June, 1776, slaves from several plantations in the Baton Rouge region also "Laid a Skime to put there masters to Death."[48] Three slaves belonging to planter William Dunbar played leading roles in the plot. Dunbar, who seemed unable to comprehend the inherent brutality of human bondage, or why well-treated slaves might resort to rebellion, was shocked to learn of the conspiracy. "Of what avail is kindness & good usage when rewarded by such ingratitude," he bemoaned. It was true that "they were kept under due subordination & obliged to do their duty in respect to plantation work," he added, but only one of his three accused slaves had ever "received a stroke of the whip." One of Dunbar's slaves committed suicide after being confronted about his involvement; a trial condemned three other men to death and prescribed lighter punishments for several more of the guilty.[49]

In 1795, the whole country around Point Coupée, on the western side of the river, was convulsed by a similar plot involving considerably more black conspirators. Originating on the plantation of Julien Poydras, the plot understandably aroused the fears of settlers east of the river as well. Disagreement between its leaders over the beginning date of the rebellion led to its discovery and a deadly confrontation with the local militia. A number of the rebels were killed outright; fifty others were tried and convicted, sixteen of whom were hastily executed.[50]

Although territorial Mississippi experienced no major problems with slave uprisings, the region's history had clearly revealed that such occurrences were possible. Frequent outbreaks of hysteria generated by news of conspiracies, real and imagined, near and afar, were a notable part of life in the slaveholding South, particularly in the densely populated black belts. Until the institution finally ended, white Mississippi's fears about violent slave resistance remained ever present. But the fact that no actual rebellion occurred—in either the territorial or later antebellum period—did not mean total black acquiescence in their status. Violent resistance was an act of desperation for often desperate men; in a region where the dominant group's police power was as great as it was, revolt was bound to fail and retribution was sure to be brutal. Slaves knew this and hence found numerous other ways to confront their oppression. Perhaps no defiant activity gave them greater release from their suffering than running away.

However temporary and dangerous it might have been, running away was an attractive form of resistance. Neither fear of the unfamiliar wilderness nor concern over the unusually harsh punishment that awaited returnees served effectively to deter their flight. So many slaves took this action that it became a source of considerable complaint and great cost to their masters.[51] In provincial Mississippi, fugitive slaves often found long-term refuge among the Indian enemies of the French. Naturally, such practices drove a larger wedge between badly strained red and white relationships in the region. A better situation for the fugitive was asylum in the long-standing, well-organized, and well-armed maroon villages similar to one established in the forest around New Orleans during the Revolutionary War era.[52] However, these kinds of independent slave camps did not exist in areas of today's Mississippi. Perhaps all that any fugitive slave in the Mississippi country could reasonably expect from running away was the satisfaction of venting anger and frustration and perhaps enjoying a brief respite from the daily rigors of bondage. Captured by the slave patrol or driven back to the plantation because of hunger or the elements, the runaway normally accepted punishment and learned to cope as best he or she could with the ordeal.

The Africans' burden of slavery was not so heavy that it precluded their discharge of other duties and responsibilities in the region. This was especially true in providing for colonial defense. In provincial Mississippi where there were few men, black or white, the African played a vital military role against both internal and external enemies. White authorities were certainly apprehensive about arming the slaves, but in times of critical needs the issue was less troublesome.

Such a case was evident in the French retaliation against the Natchez Indians and their Chickasaw allies. At least fifteen Africans participated in Governor Périer's initial but unsuccessful expedition against the Natchez. They acquitted themselves well in battle. In his report to Paris authorities, the governor praised these men for their "deeds of suprizing valor." He added that the only reason more slaves had not replaced more regular French soldiers, whose performance had been "so bad," was that the Africans were "expensive and so necessary" for Louisiana's economic advancement.[53] Africans fought in the subsequent campaigns that eventually subdued the Natchez, but their greatest numerical role in Louisiana's Indian wars occurred against the Chickasaws in northeastern Mississippi. Chickasaw-French relations, which had never been friendly, grew steadily worse after the Chickasaw gave refuge to many of the Natchez Indians involved in the Fort Rosalie massacre. After his return as governor in 1732, Bienville launched a major campaign to destroy the Chickasaw. There were 140 Africans, both slave and free, in the force that attacked the Chickasaw villages in the spring of 1736. At the Battle of Ackia, these blacks suffered with Bienville his most humiliating defeat as the Indians routed his entire command. But Captain Simon, a free black officer in command of a company of free Negroes, came under special praise for his brave conduct in the battle and the disorganized retreat.[54] Clearly, then, Africans played an important military role in French Mississippi, and at least in these cases, it had little to do with the provincial policy of "divide and rule."

Africans in Spanish Louisiana also gave a good accounting of themselves in the military. Although their combat activity was minimal, a significant number of free blacks played a major role in the Spanish defeat of the British in the Gulf region during the American Revolution. Organized by the Spanish governor-general in New Orleans, Bernardo de Gálvez, a company of free blacks was among the force that captured the British forts at Manchac and Natchez. In campaigns outside of the Mississippi country where combat was more intense, these black soldiers from the Mississippi region won acclaim for their valor and devotion to duty.[55]

Unlike the French and the Spanish, neither British nor American officials in provincial and territorial Mississippi employed blacks in the military. It is true that both England and the United States armed slaves and free blacks in the Revolutionary War and in the War of 1812, but their activity in these conflicts generally occurred outside of the Mississippi country. An exception was Andrew Jackson's use of free black battalions at the Battle of New Orleans at the end of the War of 1812. These troops were made up of free black residents of the Crescent City, which by this period had long ago ceased identification with territorial Mississippi. Mississippians in the territorial era were certainly not willing to see armed weapons in the hands of the black population.

Clearly, the life of the African in colonial and territorial Mississippi was not all despair and hopelessness. Black life had much to do with what ordinary people did who were neither black nor enslaved. Their work was their most obvious activity, but along with their sweat they shed blood and displayed bravery. Africans in these eras also created a community separate from their work environment that did much in helping them to cope and to resist becoming totally dehumanized. In this respect they found strength through their families, enjoyment in their leisure, and spiritual renewal in their religion. These were not outlets peculiar to Africans; in many ways, their lives paralleled the lives of white frontier people throughout the Lower Mississippi Valley. To be sure, as slaves, their burdens were greater, their labor more demanding, and their aspirations largely unfulfilled; but these shortcomings never broke the spirit of the vast majority of these people. Their inferior condition deviated considerably from the circumstances of the whites whom most of them served. That status, however, can never diminish their monumental impact on the development and evolution of Mississippi and its surrounding environs.

NOTES

1. Charles E. Gayarré, *History of Louisiana: French Dominion*, 4 vols. (New Orleans: Armand and Hawkins, 1885), 1:100, 254; Marcel Giraud, *A History of French Louisiana: the Company of the Indies, 1723–1731*, 5 vols., trans. by Brian Pearce (Baton Rouge: Louisiana State University Press, 1991), 3:118; Bienville to Jerome Phélypeaux Pontchartain, July 28, 1706, in *Mississippi Provincial Archives, French Dominion*, 5 vols.; vols. 1–3 ed. and trans. Dunbar Rowland and Albert Godfrey Sanders (Jackson: Press of the Mississippi Department of Archives and History, 1927), vols. 4–5 ed. Patricia Kay Galloway (1984), 2:23, 28. Hereafter cited as *MPAFD*, by volume.

2. Pontchartrain to Bienville, May 10, 1710, *MPAFD*, 3:141.

3. Périer to the Abbé Roguet, May 12, 1728, *MPAFD*, 2:573–574; Périer and Salmon to Maurepas, December 5, 1731, *MPAFD*, 4:86

4. The Council of Louisiana to the Directors of the Company of the Indies, August 28, 1725, *MPAFD*, 2: 492; Quotation from Giraud, *French Louisiana*, 4:118. There were a few African slaves in Louisiana during its initial years, but they were hardly noticeable. By 1712, for example, there were only ten in the province. See N.M. Miller Surrey, *The Commerce of Louisiana During the French Regime, 1699–1763* (New York: Longmans, Green, & Co., 1916), 231.

5. Walter G. Howell, "The French Period, 1699–1763," in *A History of Mississippi*, 2 vols., ed. Richard A. McLemore (Hattiesburg: University & College Press of Mississippi, 1973), 1:127; Surrey, *Commerce of Louisiana*, 232; D. Clayton James, *Antebellum Natchez* (Baton Rouge: Louisiana State University Press, 1968), 8.

6. Father Raphael to the Abbé Roguet, Dec 29, 1726, *MPAFD*, 2:527; Memoir on Louisiana by Bienville, *MPAFD*, 3:520–522; Surrey, *Commerce of Louisiana*, 232, 241; John Ray Skates, *Mississippi: A Bicentennial History* (New York: Norton, 1979), 29.

7. Périer and de la Chaise to the Directors of the Company of the Indies, November 24, 1727, *MPAFD*, 2:561; Vaudreuil and Michel to Rouillé, May 19, 1751, *MPAFD*, 5:80; Surrey, *Commerce of Louisiana*, 74–75.

8. James, *Antebellum Natchez*, 7–8; Giraud, *French Louisiana*, 4:122–125.

9. Giraud, *French Louisiana*, 4:125; Gayarré, *History of Louisiana*, I, 242.

10. Gayarré, *History of Louisiana*, 1:532–539.

11. *Ibid*. Another major departure found in Bienville's *Code Noir* was a provision that gave emancipated slaves in the colony the same privileges and rights as were given other Frenchmen. Whether such provisions were practiced as written is highly debatable. Louisiana was a large colony and obviously not always adequately policed during this era; it would not have been difficult to get around many of the liberal provisions included in Bienville's code.

12. Antoine Simon Le Page du Pratz, *The History of Louisiana* (1775; reprint, New Orleans: Pelican Publishing Company, 1947), 73–87; John F.H. Claiborne, *Mississippi as a Province, Territory, and State* (Jackson: Power and Barksdale, 1880), 113; Skates, *Mississippi*, 7.

13. Claiborne, *Mississippi as a Province*, 106–108; James, *Antebellum Natchez*, 17; Robert E.A. Fabel, *The Economy of British West Florida, 1763–1783* (Tuscaloosa: University of Alabama Press, 1988), 7–8, 22.

14. Quoted in Fabel, *Economy of British West Florida*, 23.

15. Cecil Johnson, *British West Florida*, 1763–1783 (1943), 158.

16. Claiborne, *Mississippi as a Province*, 105–106; Fabel, *Economy of British West Florida*, 29–36; Robert V. Haynes, *The Natchez District and The American Revolution* (Jackson: University Press of Mississippi, 1976), 18.

17. Haynes, *Natchez District*, 29–32; Johnson, *British West Florida*, 146–147, 149, 184.

18. Johnson, *British West Florida*, 177; Fabel, *Economy of British West Florida*, 44–45.

19. Robert R. Rea, "Planters and Plantations in British West Florida," *Alabama Review*, 29 (July, 1976) 228; Eron Rowland, ed., *Life, Letters, and Papers of William Dunbar, 1749–1810* (Jackson: Press of the Mississippi Historical Society, 1930), 24, 40, 70–71.

20. Bernard Romans, *A Concise Natural History of East and West Florida* (1775; reprint, New Orleans: Pelican Publishing Co., 1961), 78.

21. James, *Antebellum Natchez*, 19.

22. Romans, *Natural History*, 78.

23. Robert R. Rea and Milo B. Howard Jr., comps. *The Minutes, Journals, and Acts of the General Assembly of British West Florida* (University: University of Alabama Press, 1979), 330–336; 342–347. In the course of six months in 1767, the West Florida assembly enacted two slave codes. This paper addresses the first law. The second code was clearly more stringent than the first, and perhaps largely for this reason, the London government invalidated it and declared the original law in force again.

24. Fabel, *Economy of British West Florida*, 24.

25. Haynes, *Natchez District*, 51–152.

26. James, *Antebellum Natchez*, 41–42, 45; Jack D.L. Holmes., "A Spanish Province," in McLemore, ed. *History of Mississippi*, 1:169.

27. Jack D.L. Holmes, *Gayoso, The Life of a Spanish Governor in the Mississippi Valley, 1789–1799* (Baton Rouge: Louisiana State University Press, 1965), 90–94; John Hebron Moore, *Agriculture in Antebellum Mississippi* (New York: Bookman Associates, 1958), 18–19.

28. Skates, *Mississippi*, 35; John K. Bettersworth, *Mississippi: A History* (Austin: Steck Co., 1959), 111.

29. Holmes, "A Spanish Province," 167.

30. Moore, *Agriculture in Antebellum Mississippi*, 21–22; John Boles, *Black Southerners, 1619–1869* (Lexington: University of Kentucky Press, 1983), 59. Benjamin Wailes, an important planter and personage of the old Natchez district claims that the gin was "constructed almost entirely" by this slave. See Benjamin L.C. Wailes, *Report on the Agriculture and Geology of Mississippi, Embracing a Sketch of the Social and Natural History of the State*, (Philadelphia, Miss.: E. Barksdale, 1854), 167.

31. Dunbar quoted in Claiborne, *Mississippi as a Province*, 143, 144.

32. Charles Lowery, "The Great Migration to the Mississippi Territory, 1798–1819," in *A Mississippi Reader*, ed. John E. Gonzales (Jackson: Mississippi Historical Society, 1980), 74–75; Skates, *Mississippi*, 66.

33. Robert L. Jenkins, "African-Americans on the Natchez Trace, 1800–1865," *Southern Quarterly*, 29 (summer, 1991): 49–52.

34. John Hebron Moore, *The Emergence of the Cotton Kingdom in the Old South-*

west (Baton Rouge: Louisiana State University Press, 1988), 77–78; Boles, *Black Southerners*, 78–79.

35. Charles S. Sydnor, *Slavery in Mississippi* (Baton Rouge: Louisiana State University Press, 1933), 6–8, 178–179; Joseph Holt Ingraham *The South-West By a Yankee*, 2 vols. (New York: Harper & Brothers, 1935), 2:249.

36. Moore, *Cotton Kingdom*, 262–263; Charles S. Sydnor, "The Free Negro in Mississippi Before the Civil War," *American Historical Review*, 32 (July, 1927): 769–788.

37. Anderson Hutchinson, comp. *Code of Mississippi. 1798–1848* (Jackson: State Printers, 1848), 510–542. Unless otherwise noted, this section on the laws regulating slave activity is derived from this code.

38. Alfred H. Stone, "The Early Slave Laws of Mississippi," *Publications of the Mississippi Historical Society*, 2 (1899): 135.

39. Hutchinson, *Mississippi Code*, 519.

40. William K. Scarborough, "Heartland of the Cotton Kingdom," in McLemore, ed. *History of Mississippi*, 1:329.

41. Ibid.

42. Governor Winthrop Sargent, Circular Letter to Slave-holders, November 16, 1800, in *Mississippi Territorial Archives*, 1798–1803, ed. Dunbar Rowland (Nashville: Brandon Printing Company, 1905), 311.

43. Beauchamp to Maurepas, November 5, 1731, *MPAFD*, 4:82.

44. du Pratz, *History of Louisiana*, 77–78.

45. Gayarré, *History of Louisiana*, 1:415

46. Périer to Maurepas, March 18, 1730, *MPAFD*, 1:64; Gayarré, *History of Louisiana*, 1:422–423; William S. Willis Jr., "Divide and Rule: Red, White, and Black in the Southeast" in *Red, White, and Black; Symposium on Indians in the Old South*, ed. Charles M. Hudson (Athens, Ga.: Southern Anthropological Society, 1971), 106.

47. Quoted in Willis, "Red, White and Black," 106.

48. John Fitzpatrick to John Stephenson, July 2, 1776, in *The Merchant of Manchac; the Letterbook of John Fitzpatrick, 1768–1790*, ed. Margaret Fisher Dalrymple (Baton Rouge: Louisiana State University Press, 1978), 204.

49. Rowland, *William Dunbar*, 27.

50, Francois-Xavier Martin, *The History of Louisiana, from the Earliest Period* (1827; reprint, Gretna, La.: Pelican Publishing Company, 1975), 266.

51. See for example, references to runaways in several letters in Dalrymple, *Merchant of Manchac*, 111, 131, 132, 235, 291–292; and Rowland, *William Dunbar*, 46–47.

52. Willis, "Divide and Rule," 102–103; Joe Gray Taylor, *Negro Slavery in Louisiana* (Baton Rouge: The Louisiana Historical Association, 1963), 16–17.

53. Périer to Maurepas, March 18, 1730, *MPAFD*, 1:70.

54. D'ron d' Artaguette to Maurepas, June 24, 1731, *MPAFD*, 4:78; Howell, "The French Period," 130–132; Roland C. McConnell, *Negro Troops in Antebellum Loui-*

siana: A History of the Battalion of Free Men of Color (Baton Rouge: Louisiana State University Press, 1968), 10–12.

55. McConnell, *Negro Troops*, 17–21.

SUGGESTED READINGS

Bancroft, Frederic. *Slave-Trading in the Old South.* Baltimore: H.J. Furst, 1931.

Berlin, Ira. *Slaves Without Masters: The Free Negro in the Antebellum South.* New York: Pantheon Books, 1974.

Blassingame, John. *The Slave Community: Plantation Life in the Antebellum South.* New York: Oxford University Press, 1979.

Boles, John, ed. *Masters and Slaves in the House of the Lord: Race and Religion in the American South, 1740–1870.* Lexington: University of Kentucky Press, 1988.

Botkin, Benjamin A., ed. *Lay My Burden Down: A Folk History of Slavery.* Chicago: University of Chicago Press, 1945.

Cohen, David W., and Jack P. Greene, eds. *Neither Slave Nor Free: The Freedmen of African Descent in the Slave Societies of the New World.* Baltimore: John Hopkins University Press, 1972.

Davis, Edwin and William Ransom Hogan. *The Barber of Natchez.* Baton Rouge: Louisiana State University Press, 1954,

Feldstein, Stanley. *Once a Slave: The Slaves' View of Slavery.* New York: W. Morrow, 1971.

Fisher, Miles Mark. *Negro Slave Songs in the United States.* Ithaca: Cornell University Press, 1953.

Fox-Genovese, Elizabeth. *Within the Plantation Household: Black and White Women of the Old South.* Chapel Hill: University of North Carolina Press, 1988.

Genovese, Eugene D. *Roll, Jordan, Roll: The World the Slaves Made.* New York: Pantheon Books, 1974.

————. *From Rebellion to Revolution: Afro-American Slave Revolts in the Making of the New World.* Baton Rouge: Louisiana State University Press, 1979.

Gutman, Herbert. *The Black Family in Slavery and Freedom, 1750–1925.* New York: Pantheon Books, 1976.

Hall, Gwendolyn Midlo. *The Afro-Creole Culture of Louisiana: Formation During the Eighteenth Century.* Baton Rouge: Louisiana State University, 1991.

Huggins, Nathan Irvin. *Black Odyssey: The Afro-American Ordeal in Slavery.* New York: Vintage Books, 1977.

Jordan, Winthrop D. *White Over Black: American Attitudes Towards the Negro, 1550–1812.* Chapel Hill: University of North Carolina Press, 1968.

Kipple, Kenneth F. and Virginia H. King. *Another Dimension to the Black Diaspora: Diet, Disease, and Racism.* (Cambridge: Cambridge University Press, 1981.

Levine, Lawrence W. *Black Culture and Black Consciousness: Afro-American Folk Thought From Slavery to Freedom*. New York: Oxford University Press, 1977.

Litwack, Leon F. *Been in the Storm So Long: The Aftermath of Slavery*. New York: Alfred A. Knopf, 1979.

Mannix, Daniel P. and Malcolm Cowley. *Black Cargoes: A History of the Atlantic Slave Trade, 1515–1815*. New York: Viking Press, 1962.

Nash, Gary P. *Red, White, and Black: The People of Early America*. Englewood Cliffs, N.J.: Prentice Hall, 1974.

Newton, James E., and Ronald L. Lewis, eds. *The Other Slaves: Mechanics, Artisans, and Craftsmen*. Boston: G. K. Hall, 1978.

Owen, Leslie H. *This Species of Property: Slave Life and Culture in the Old South*. New York: Oxford University Press, 1976.

Price, Richard ed. *Maroon Societies: Rebel Slave Communities in the Americas*. Garden City, N.Y.: Doubleday, 1976.

Quarles, Benjamin. *The Negro in the American Revolution*. Chapel Hill: University of North Carolina Press, 1961.

Raboteau, Albert J. *Slave Religion: The "Invisible Institution" in the Antebellum South*. New York: Oxford University Press, 1976.

Rawick, George P. *From Sundown to Sunup: The Making of the Black Community*. Westport, Conn.: Greenwood Press, 1972.

Rawley, James A. *The Transatlantic Slave Trade: A History*. New York: W.W. Norton Co, 1981.

Sobel, Mechal. *Trabelin' On: The Slave Journey to an Afro-Baptist Faith*. Westport, Conn.: Greenwood Press, 1979.

Stampp, Kenneth. *The Peculiar Institution*. New York: Alfred A, Knopf, 1956.

Starobin, Robert S. *Industrial Slavery in The Old South*. New York: Oxford University Press, 1976.

Wade, Richard. *Slavery in the Cities: The South 1820–1860*. New York: Oxford University Press, 1964.

Webber, Thomas L. *Deep Like the Rivers: Education in the Slave Quarter Community, 1831–1865*. New York: W.W. Norton, 1978.

Williamson, Joel. *New People: Miscegenation and Mulattoes in the United States*. New York: Free Press, 1980.

White, Deborah Gray. *Ar'n't I a Woman? Female Slaves in the Plantation South*. New York: W.W. Norton, 1985.

PART THREE

THE CONTEMPORARY ETHNIC SCENE
A Photo Essay

Ethnic Mississippi 1992

D.C. Young and Stephen Young

> *[To know who you are], you have to have roots to be proud of.*
> —*Queenie Nossour, Vicksburg*

In recent years, few subjects have aroused more controversy than the questions of ethnicity and identity in American life. As Americans look once more at their past, this time taking the long view of five hundred years since Columbus's voyages, they are asking questions which have plagued and defined this country since its inception. Much of the history of the encounters between indigenous Native Americans and European, African, and later Asian newcomers is the story of cultural misunderstanding. Earlier essays in this volume detail much of this history. This essay, the photographs and text together, will show the diversity of contemporary Mississippi.

Is there an "American" culture into which all newcomers are to be subsumed once ties to their various "Old Worlds" are severed? After a generation or two, is everyone expected to become a "full-fledged American"? And why do third and subsequent generations often realign themselves with their first-generation ancestors? What of the phenomenon of "ethnicity by consent"—

rediscovering one's roots and consciously reacquiring ethnic characteristics and identifying with one's cultural heritage?

It appears that our national unity is paradoxical: America has always been a chorus of many independent voices. The reason may be that culture is more resistant to change than the "melting pot" mythology once taught. Ethnic patterns of thought, religion, folk customs, and cuisine continue to survive—even to flourish. This holds true not only for recent immigrants but also for groups that have been here for generations.

The understanding of ethnicity must begin with the concept that diversity is essential to the American way of life. Diversity is at the heart of all democratic institutions; but in the United States, the world's most polycultural country, diversity means more than civil and political rights. It also means the right to live one's life free of the coercive restraints and conformities that may be imposed by the majority.

The following essay and photographs will identify some of the ethnic communities existing in Mississippi today and focus on the patterns of ethnic identity and community in the state. It is not intended to be a comprehensive history of groups. The research is based predominantly on personal interviews and is still in progress.

A word about ethnicity: an ethnic group is any group which shares common beliefs and patterns of living—religion, customs, literature, cuisine, language. Many people believe that once immigrants arrive in the United States they can either remain loyal to their ethnic culture and isolate themselves from American life, or they can give up their ethnic traits for a common American culture. According to the melting pot theory, after a few generations the differences among various groups usually become so mild that group solidarity disintegrates and members freely interact with others. Yet the reality of assimilation is much more complex. Cultural forms are as tough as the gnarled roots of ancient trees. Though they may appear dead, they put out growth. Ethnic groups often seek a middle course between the extremes of isolation and total merging with the standardized national culture. The compromises and adaptations of such cultural adjustments are apparent in the groups examined here.

Native Americans

By the turn of the twentieth century, the Choctaws remained the only indigenous tribe in Mississippi despite pressures to relocate or to assimilate.

Despite governmental and social pressure, Mississippi Choctaw culture did not decline, as photographs taken in 1907 by M. R. Harrington for a Smithsonian ethnographic study prove.[1] (See plate 1.) The Choctaws' ability to keep their essential cultural practices intact was undoubtedly assisted by the establishment of a Choctaw reservation in East Central Mississippi in 1918.

The sturdy nature of cultural forms is nowhere more evident than in the life of the Choctaws today. Most Choctaws speak their native language as a first language, and Choctaw schools are bilingual. The policy of the Mississippi Choctaw tribal government, headed by Chief Phillip Martin, is "Choctaw self-determination," sustained by maintaining Choctaw traditional customs. Despite the existence of a separate government and language, today not even the most rural Choctaw is isolated from mass culture. Today the Choctaws actively seek to balance mass media with their own. For example, the tribe's communication center has state-of-the-art equipment and classes which teach television production so that the Choctaws may develop programs about their own lives.

Choctaws also maintain their ethnicity through persistent tribal support for traditional culture. Although the tribe operates numerous enterprises to provide jobs and an up-to-date standard of living, tribal leaders also know that traditional crafts, for example, are vital in keeping Choctaws independent. Every year at the Choctaw Indian Fair held during the first week of July at the reservation in Neshoba County, many basket makers, seamstresses, and bead workers display and demonstrate their crafts. These skills and talents are not "tourist" art—far from it. Many Choctaws use swamp cane baskets every day and normally wear traditional styles of clothing. In the rural areas, away from the reservation, many farmers' wives still wear cotton Choctaw dresses. One Choctaw farmer, Barney Wesley, lives a traditional Choctaw lifestyle, maintaining old customs of gardening and food preparation and serving as a counselor and herbalist to a wide community in the Upper Pearl River area around Nanih Waiya. Melvin Henry, who retired from farming a few years ago is still active at his white oak basketry, both for the satisfaction of the work itself and for the small income it brings. His methods have changed little from those he learned from his father, Albert Henry.

In many ways, the Choctaws sustain a middle course, maintaining a lifestyle that is different from the national standard while at the same time being completely "American."

The British: Anglo-Welsh-Scots-Irish

The survival of ethnic traits among the descendants of the state's most numerous immigrants—settlers from the British Isles—constitute today the best example of both ethnicity of descent and ethnicity by consent. In the early years of the history of the state, Irish settlers constituted a significant proportion of the newcomers. A survey of the gravestones in Jackson's Greenwood Cemetery will show that many of the city's early citizens were descendants of the "Old Sod" of Ireland. One headstone in a Greenwood cemetery reads, "Sacred to the Memory of Robert Farrell." Another reads: "A native of County Meath, Ireland. Died May 1881, aged 80 years. Also his wife Marcella, a native of County Meath, Ireland, d. Feb. 1872, aged 73." Jackson early on had an established Roman Catholic congregation, and many of its Irish pastors are also buried in Greenwood Cemetery. Names like Hardy, Toole, Monaghan, O'Leary, Sullivan, and Shaughnessy abound.

According to David Hackett Fischer in his book, *Albion's Seed*, the folkways of settlers from the British Isles continue to influence their descendants and shape popular beliefs.[2] In Mississippi, which was settled by hardy and individualistic persons from Ireland, Scotland, and northern England, this has meant highly individualistic attitudes toward government, social relations, labor unions, and religion.

Historian Grady McWhiney also notes that the South has been culturally dominated by the Celts who settled there in great numbers. McWhiney suggests that this accounts for certain traits in Mississippi: a pastoral society and a disdain for the hard work of tillage (what McWhiney calls "an orientation toward leisure"—hunting, fishing, drinking, and horseracing being especially popular pursuits); unpretentiousness in manners and living habits combined with hospitality; and self-sufficiency, sometimes to the point of being reclusive. According to McWhiney, "southerners and Celts were oral and aural people, who delighted in oratory . . . they were also clannish, superstitious, and more emotional than rational."[3]

These general traits aside, has a distinctively Celtic ethnicity survived in Mississippi? Ethnicity of descent survives in Bassfield, a community in south central Mississippi. St. Peter's Catholic Church in Bassfield presents a strongly Irish demeanor and traces the history of the Irish community in the area as far back as the 1850s, when Michael O'Rourke, a native of Ireland, settled in the country north of Columbia. He and his family were joined there by other Irish immigrants and eventually formed the parish of St. Peter in Bassfield, which, from 1927 to 1957, had a parochial school operated by the Sisters of Mercy.[4] Another example of Irishness by consent is the Hibernian Society of the Gulf Coast, an association of Irish descendants organized in recent years which sponsors a number of events each year.

Africans

African Mississippians, descendants of African laborers brought to the South in the eighteenth and nineteenth centuries, retain many ethnic characteristics. African folk traditions persist in food customs, styles of dress, music, and the visual arts.

In rural areas of the state, African Mississippians practice arts and crafts derived from African traditions. Mary B. Gholar, a native of Oakdale, makes white oak baskets which she markets at a fruit stand on U. S. Highway 49 near Collins. Many African Mississippians who live in urban areas also retain their African identity. African knowledge and use of tradition is represented in the Smith-Robertson Museum and Cultural Center in Jackson, where exhibits feature the artistic contributions of African Mississippians. Perhaps one of the most widely known of the African Mississippi traditions is the Delta blues music, which is based on African principles of rhythm and tonality. Mississippi has produced such musicians as B. B. King, Little Milton, Son Thomas, Bobby Whalen, and Booba Barnes. Throughout the state, various communities and groups sponsor blues festivals. One of the most recognized festivals is held annually in Greenville. The Carnegie Library in Clarksdale now houses the Mississippi Delta Blues Museum, which has received international support and recognition, and the Center for the Study of Southern Culture at the University of Mississippi maintains an impressive blues archive.

In Bay St. Louis there is another side to the African experience in Mississippi—that of black Creoles. The term "black Creole" is popularly used today by those who claim both African descent and French or Spanish lineage.

The Roman Catholic parish of St. Rose de Lima in Bay St. Louis serves as the nucleus and cultural home for most black Creoles on the coast, many of whom are descendants of the people who settled Hancock County in the nineteenth century. The black Mississippi Creoles who came from South Louisiana often prospered in business, developing, for instance, a thriving seafood packing plant complete with its own fishing schooners. They readily established easy relations with whites in the area from the earliest days. After racial tensions escalated in the early twentieth century with the imposition of rigid Jim Crow laws, the active participation of black Creoles was no longer tolerated in business, social, or religious spheres and the St. Rosa de Lima Church was founded primarily for their worship.

The traditions of Creole life are still strong in the neighborhood surrounding St. Rose de Lima, which also includes descendants of the Choctaws. The parish priest, Father Kenneth Hamilton, directed the recent renovation of the church and its transformation into a sanctuary devoted to the appreciation of cultural diversity. The themes of African religious belief are represented, according to Father Hamilton, in the use of trees—in the construction of the altar and podium out of huge driftwood trunks, and in the painting behind the altar of Jesus ascending to Heaven through the branches of a live oak (see photo 36). African motifs and colors in altar fabrics are repeated in the priest's robes and in the sash worn by the ascending Jesus. Most impressive, however, is the depiction of Jesus as a multi-racial embodiment of all humanity. All of the symbolism of Father Hamilton's church represents the ideal of humanity as a community responsible for every member—a belief which has strong roots in the African tradition.

French

The earliest European settlers on the Gulf coast, the French, established patterns of living that have lasted through today. The mid-winter carnival season which culminates with Mardi Gras and the annual blessing of the fishing fleet are notable examples. Perhaps the most distinctive of French ethnic traditions in Mississippi, however, is that of boat building.

To trace the story of the Biloxi schooner is to trace much of the history of the Gulf coast. The first fishing boats on the coast had shallow drafts which could easily ply the waters of the Mississippi Sound. Sometime in the nineteenth century, these early French designs were augmented by larger and faster designs perhaps copied from the Chesapeake Bay fishing schooners. The French Fountain family of Biloxi were responsible for some of the coast's swiftest schooner designs, and passed their boat-building knowledge to incoming immigrants, primarily the Slavonians.

Acadian French

Because of its proximity to New Orleans, the coast has seen the general influence of French culture reinforced and renewed. Families trace their genealogies and maintain a sense of pride and identity with their heritage, but the sense of a particularly French ethnic community now exists primarily among the Acadian French.

Louisiana's Acadian French, or Cajuns, began to migrate to the Gulf coast around 1910, drawn by the promise of employment in the seafood industry. Descendants of the Acadian refugees who had come to southwest Louisiana from Canada in the mid-eighteenth century, the Cajuns hold tenaciously to their ethnic customs. Many have stayed in the seafood industry as fishermen, netmakers, and processing plant owners.[5]

Although most Mississippi Acadians have become somewhat Americanized in their language and culture, ties to the Acadian way of life remain strong. Family reunions in Louisiana today bring together families separated when members moved to another location, and in the early days it was not uncommon for deceased Cajuns to be returned to Louisiana for burial. They remain loyal to their unique music, with its characteristic rhythms and use of fiddles and accordions. Because there are no Cajun bands on the coast, they must be brought in from Louisiana for the dances, called *fais do do*, sponsored by the Acadian's Fleur de Lis Society. The *fais do do* is so named because the children are put to sleep early so the adults can get on with revelry.[6]

Cajun cuisine has become internationally famous, and for Acadians on the coast, authentic Cajun cooking is an important statement of identity, redefined with every dish. There may be disagreements among cooks about proportions of ingredients in gumbo, but there is little doubt that there is a right way—the Acadian way—to prepare it.

Hispanics

During the colonial period, the Gulf coast attracted Spanish immigrants such as the Balius family who found the coast compatible with their Latin sensibilities. For three generations the Baliuses have been engaged in the production of ornamental ironwork, following a tradition which has given the Gulf coast and New Orleans much of their special character.

In recent years, the Spanish have been joined by Hispanic Americans. According to Miguel Saavedra, the largest group on the coast may be the Mexicans. Saavedra, who first lived in Biloxi in 1968 while stationed at Keesler Air Force Base, liked the coastal area and moved back when he retired. In Biloxi he found a growing number of families from Mexico, Honduras, Colombia, Costa Rica, and Venezuela, and helped organize the Hispanic Cultural Society.

Many Hispanic people have been drawn to the Coast by Keesler, while others work for the Ingalls shipyards in Pascagoula. Like Saavedra, these people often find the coast's ambience compatible to that of their homeland.[7]

In a recent interview, Saavedra speculated about ethnicity. "The current generation," he said, "is rediscovering its heritage. My son grew up not wanting to speak Spanish, but now he lives in New Orleans and is taking [Spanish] classes. He feels that he must be part of my culture. He wants to talk to me in my native tongue."[8]

Most Hispanic families on the coast prepare foods of their native lands, and their cuisines can be markedly different. "The first week of October has been proclaimed Hispanic Heritage Week by the city of Biloxi," said Saavedra, "and at our festival there will be at least four different kinds of Spanish rice!"[9]

Religious observance is important for most Hispanic families, and several Catholic churches on the coast conduct Mass in Spanish. There is a house-to-house Rosary Society in Long Beach. "Back home," said Saavedra, "it was the custom for people to gather and say the rosary every night. This is a way of continuing the tradition."[10]

The Hispanic Association on the coast stages several festivals each year, including a *Cinco de Mayo* celebration which has its origins in the overthrow of Spanish imperial control of Latin America.

Hispanic influence is not only present on the Coast but also in other parts of Mississippi. A Roman Catholic church in Cleveland annually stages a procession in observance of the Virgin of Guadalupe, patron saint of Mexico; a Catholic church in Jackson provides Mass in Spanish every Sunday afternoon; and all across the Delta there are tamale stands, which often do a prodigious business, a result, perhaps, of the popularity of the dish with Mexican farm workers brought to the region years ago but by now a custom long taken up by everyone.[11]

Slavonians

The Slavonians began arriving in Biloxi before 1900. Most fled their native Dalmatian coast towns and villages to avoid military service under hated Austrian commanders or in search of better economic opportunities. One family sent for another until the workers' housing—wood frame shanties thrown up by the packing plants—was crowded with Slavonian Catholics. Most began their lives in America as seafood plant workers and fishermen, but the second and third generations sought opportunities elsewhere.[12]

Today the ethnic tradition of boat building is carried on by two boat builders, Neilius Covacevich and Bob Holland. Covacevich and his older brother, Tony Jack Covacevich, worked for many years in partnership with their father, Jacky Jack Covacevich. According to Tony Jack, over five hundred vessels were constructed in the Covacevich yard on Back Bay. One of these was the championship Biloxi schooner, the *Mary Margaret*. Keeping this boat building tradition alive today is the Biloxi Seafood Industry Museum, located on the tip of Point Cadet. The museum has sponsored the construction of two schooners, one of which, the *Glenn L. Swetman*, has been completed by Bob Holland. Neil Covacevich's boat is nearing completion, waiting only for sufficient funding. The goal is to revive the tradition of the "Race of the White Wings," the Biloxi schooner race held annually in the days when the fishing fleet consisted entirely of schooners. The last of these races was held around 1935 (nobody can agree on the exact year), as the schooners began to fall victim to motor–powered trawlers.[13]

Ethnic customs among the Slavonian community are kept cohesive and functioning mostly because of the Slavic Benevolent Association, founded in 1913, and its women's auxiliary. The Association's hall is the scene of holiday celebrations, wedding receptions, and festivals. The St. Nicola shrine in front of the Association's headquarters is engraved with the names of all the Slavonian families who have settled on the coast.

Although few Slavonians speak in their native tongue, there is a choral and dance group which performs Slavonian folk music and dresses in Slavonian costume. At their programs, they always sing "God Bless America" in Slavonian to point out that while they are good Americans, they want their children to appreciate their native culture. Many of the Mississippi Slavonians have returned to the Dalmatian coast to visit the villages and towns from which their grandparents and great–grandparents came.[14] Every year, a few days before Christmas, the women's auxiliary of the Slavic Benevolent Association gathers at the lodge hall to prepare *pusharatas*, a kind of fried pastry. Over five hundred dozen pastries are prepared and sold to support the maintenance of the association. The auxiliary also prepares a cookbook with many Slavonian recipes.

The persistent closeness of family ties between two ethnic groups, the Acadians and the Slavonians, may be illustrated by the story of the Broussards. When Neville "Tee Jean" Broussard, an Acadian fisherman, began courting Lou Skrnich, daughter of a Slavonian family, their relationship was frowned upon. Broussard said that when he went to call on Lou he had to throw his hat in the front door before entering. If the Skrniches threw it out, he knew he was not welcome. Eventually Tee Jean and Lou married and had a family, but each was excluded from the other's ethnic organization. In recent years, however, because of the rising number of mixed marriages, the Slavic Benevolent Association and the Fleur de Lis Society have relaxed their rules and now allow spouses of members to join.[15]

Vietnamese

The Vietnamese are the most recent ethnic group to migrate to Mississippi in large numbers, settling primarily on the Gulf Coast. Most were fishermen in their native Vietnam, and many came from the same village, Vung Tau. The first Vietnamese came to the Coast in the early 1980s as oyster shuckers for the Gollott seafood plant, and they spread the word of Biloxi's similarity to the Vietnamese seacoast, encouraging others to come.

Today the Vietnamese community on the Gulf Coast numbers in the thousands (estimates range from four to ten thousand), with the majority employed in fishing or marine occupations. Some say the influx of Vietnamese fishermen revived the declining Point Cadet neighborhood and even the Biloxi seafood industry itself.

Whatever the case, the Vietnamese have become an integral part of the Coast community, at the same time retaining their customs of food, religion, and in some cases, dress. Over a dozen Vietnamese restaurants and coffee houses serve *cafe sua da*, Vietnamese–style coffee made from strong dark French roast coffee in distinctive one–cup pots and served in a glass of ice cubes with sweetened milk. One department store on the Coast carries everything necessary for living a Vietnamese life: cookware, jasmine rice, fish sauce, Peking duck, fresh oriental vegetables, joss paper, china plates, Buddhas, silk fabrics (with tailors on the premises to turn them into garments), Chinese herbal medicines, and Vietnamese rock music cassettes.

One of the Vietnamese community's most indefatigable proponents of Vietnamese culture is Minh Duc, a lawyer from Saigon who publishes a Vietnamese language newspaper, *Duyen Hai*, which carries advertisements for both Vietnamese and American businesses in Vietnamese. Minh also leads a class in cultural enrichment for children at the Division Street Community Center in Biloxi and is active in the Buddhist Temple, organizing such events as the annual Tet (lunar new year) celebration.[16]

Many Gulf Coast Vietnamese are Roman Catholic, and St. Michael's Church has a Vietnamese priest who conducts the Mass in Vietnamese. In fact, it was partly because of their faith that the Vietnamese of Vung Tau fled from North to South Vietnam in the mid-1950s after the Communist regime of Ho Chi Minh drove the French (and hence the Catholic Church) out of the country. To find the Vietnamese section of Biloxi's cemetery, one only has to locate the canopied graves decorated with carefully arranged and brilliantly colorful flowers.

Jews

Mississippi Jews are distinctly aware of their unique cultural standing, as is aptly expressed in the text for Bill Aron's photography exhibit, "Images of Southern Jewish Life." "By choice of locale and lifestyle they were southerners, but by religion and heritage they were Jews. To be a Jew in the South is to be both a southerner and a Jew. Ultimately Jews who live in Dixie are not Jewish southerners but southern Jews."[17]

For many ethnic Mississippians, the route of travel to the state has been through New Orleans, then to the Coast or up the Mississippi River. This pattern began with the Jews who settled in Natchez as early as the late eighteenth century when the town was still part of Louisiana and under Spanish control. The earliest Jewish religious services in Mississippi were held in Natchez in 1798. By the 1840s, the Jewish community in the Natchez area was large enough to support an organized congregation, B'nai Israel, founded in 1840. After that, other congregations were established in Port Gibson, Jackson, Vicksburg, Meridian, and other towns.

Immigration continued in the nineteenth and twentieth centuries as Eastern European Jews fled the oppression of the imperial governments of Austria-Hungary and Russia. Aaron Kline of the Delta town of Alligator tells of growing up in Lithuania and being brought to the United States in 1937 by his brother who had come years before. "We were like a string of pearls," Kline says of the way families often migrated. "First one would come and then bring the rest along one by one."[18]

Many Jews in Mississippi succeeded in business, and they take pride in the fact that they have been prominent in fostering civic and cultural development. In Meridian, for example, the builders of the Marks-Rothenberg department store also erected the Grand Opera House. Another Meridian landmark credited to successful Jewish businessmen was Highland Park, the city's most popular recreational attraction.[19]

The number of Jews in Mississippi has declined in recent years, and some congregations, such as the one in Port Gibson, have disbanded. The decline in the number of Jewish families has changed religious life. In Clarksdale, the temple has about twenty-three families, or about sixty members—down from its peak of approximately 150. The temple cannot afford to maintain a permanent rabbi, so for the past two years a student rabbi from Hebrew Union College in Cincinnati has come for the High Holy Days.

Even so, the Jews who remain keep many Jewish traditions alive. There is apparently a revival of traditionalism among the young, with a great interest in living according to Jewish custom.[20] "Reformed Judaism has taken back some of the traditions of the Orthodox," according to Goldie Hirshberg of Clarksdale. "It's a back–to–the–roots movement."[21] This Jewish traditionalism includes adherence to strict laws concerning preparation of food. Many grocery stores in Mississippi stock a variety of kosher foods, from matzos to pastrami. In spite of the trend toward traditional cuisine, there are also many unusual ethnic American blends, such as gumbo with matzos in place of rice.

Jews in Mississippi have not, for the most part, suffered from frequent violent anti-Semitic attacks, but they have been discriminated against. In some towns they were denied membership in the country club, and during the civil rights turbulence of the sixties, some Jewish places of worship and homes were firebombed or smeared with anti-Semitic slogans and symbols. Many Mississippians were appalled at these events, and when Temple Beth Israel in Jackson was bombed in September, 1967, a "walk of penance" was staged by a group of forty non-Jewish clergymen.[22]

Outside Jackson, near Utica, Jews created Camp Henry S. Jacobs as a retreat for Jewish youth in the South. Summer camp sessions here, beginning in 1970, attract a growing number of children each year. The camp's central location in the South has also made it a logical site for the Museum of the Southern Jewish Experience, a project founded by Macy Hart of Jackson. The museum houses artifacts of Jewish life in the South, including Torahs, breastplates, stained glass, eternal lights, and Jewish documents.[23]

Lebanese

Another ethnic group with roots in the eastern Mediterranean is the Lebanese. Immigrants from Lebanon—at that time the Christian Syrian province of the

Ottoman Empire—began arriving in Mississippi before World War I, and some as early as the 1880s. Many of them fled Lebanon to escape being conscripted into the armies of the Moslem sultan. Lebanese immigrants, in fact, were often referred to by Mississippians as Syrians. Bubba Mohammed of Inverness tells the story of his father and uncle who shipped passage to France, where they worked in Paris until they saved enough money to come to the United States. George Abraham, the earliest living Lebanese settler in Vicksburg, began as a door–to–door peddlar, "walking from Vicksburg to Yazoo City and back with a full pack of dry goods strapped to his back," eventually buying a grocery store and bringing the rest of his family to this country after World War I.[24]

Similar stories are told in Lebanese communities in Vicksburg, Jackson, and Clarksdale. Even as recently as the 1950s, Lebanese started as peddlers in the Delta. Louise and Chafik Chamoun married in Lebanon and came to the United States in 1954. Chafik worked in a grocery store for a while, then he borrowed a suitcase and received fifty dollars credit from a wholesaler of women's apparel. He peddled women's lingerie door–to–door in Tallahatchie County for years, but in the 1960s opportunities for peddling ended. Chafik and Louise opened a grocery store in Clarksdale and to supplement their income sold sandwiches made with Lebanese meat patties called kibbie. As Chafik puts it, "Once everybody tasted, everybody wanted."[25] Before long people were driving to Clarksdale from all over just for a taste of Lebanese kibbie. A year ago the Chamouns sold their grocery store and opened a restaurant which specializes in Lebanese-American food.

Maintaining food customs is one of the strongest Lebanese ethnic characteristics. Among the Lebanese, the traditional foods made with cracked wheat, parsley, or grape leaves are still popular. The Lebanese people prefer strongly spiced cuisine, according to Queenie Nossour from Vicksburg. "Lebanese food. Let me tell you about Lebanese food. If it ain't seasoned, it ain't much of anything."[26]

The Lebanese community in Vicksburg is centered around St. George Antiochan Orthodox Church. Reverend Nicholas Saikley, who served as pastor of the church for twenty–five years until his retirement last year, says that there are about 150 families associated with the church. But he points out that the Antiochan Orthodox Church itself does not have a particular ethnic identity, claiming as it does to be the original Christian church, founded in Antioch by St. Peter. Even so, most Lebanese in the Vicksburg area are involved with the church and comprise the majority of its membership.[27]

Saikley calls the Mississippi Lebanese "the most Americanized Lebanese in the U.S.—except for the food and church, of course."[28] Food customs and religion are important for maintaining ethnic characteristics, but the Lebanese also absorb those who marry into the group. According to Saikley, forty percent of the congregation of St. George's is non–Lebanese, and in all his years at St. George's he has officiated at only six weddings in which both bride and groom were Arabic. His own five daughters married non–Lebanese husbands yet remain active in the church.[29]

In the early days, Lebanese settlers were discriminated against and had to earn the respect of whites who controlled civic and financial institutions. "We were treated as blacks," according to Thomas Farris of Clarksdale.[30] The early Lebanese settlers in Clarksdale, for example, were forced to live in black neighborhoods and were able to move into other areas of the city only after a generation had passed.[31] "We were different," said Reverend Saikley. "We spoke a different language."[32] Second and third generation Lebanese have become more "American," partly by marriage, partly by adopting local language and customs, and more "Mississippian" as well.

Despite obvious Americanization, the Lebanese feel the current generation is keeping the Lebanese heritage. Ties to the old country may have weakened, but, as Chuck Abraham, a fourth-generation Lebanese from Vicksburg, said, "Heritage–wise, you'll always be what you are. It may be more difficult [to preserve traditions]. They [the children] will be more Americanized. But relationships and the closeness won't change."[33]

Italians

The earliest Italian immigrants to Mississippi arrived along the same path from New Orleans as the Jews and Lebanese. The Italians mainly settled in river towns and along the Gulf coast with a large community settling in the Delta, primarily in and around Shaw. The story of the Delta Italians differs from that of others in the state. In the late nineteenth century, Delta planters sought to replace black labor with European peasants, so they brought Italian farmers to the Delta. For the first generation life was hard. Forced labor and disease took its toll, but many immigrants were able to save enough to buy land. Today much of the land in the Delta is Italian–owned.

Italians who settled on the Gulf Coast worked in the marine and seafood industries. William Cruso was a young man and penniless when he arrived in Biloxi around the turn of the century. But it was not long before he was buying seafood from fishermen and selling it to the restaurants of Biloxi's thriving tourist industry. By the 1960s, the Cruso seafood packing plant was one of the largest on the Coast. Unfortunately, in 1969, it was, in the words of one of Cruso's daughters, "taken by [Hurricane] Camille".[34]

Around the turn of the century, the Alfonso family entered this country at New Orleans and settled in Gulfport. Here they founded the Standard Fruit Company and began importing fruit from Honduras on schooners.[35] Today the company is managed by Gino Scialdone, who is also the Italian consul in Mississippi. Scialdone is president of the local Italian–American association, which stages an annual Italian–American festival, a bocce tournament, a *Notte di Natale* at Christmas, and classes in traditional dances and in the Italian language.

Mississippi's Italians have a strong sense of community. Italian cultural societies have been organized throughout the state, including two on the coast, several in the Delta, and a state–wide association based in Jackson. George Bria from Jackson, a moving force in the Mississippi Italian–American Society, has become so interested in Italian culture that his business specializes in Italian imports and art.

Food customs are especially important to the Italians. Joseph Canizaro of Vicksburg says, "We've enjoyed the Italian way of life, especially in the cooking and the drinking."[36] Lillie Cruso Lancon introduced Italian cuisine in the form of an extraordinarily popular version of spaghetti shrimp in the family restaurant in Biloxi.

Many food customs are associated with festivals. The most popular celebration aside from Christmas is St. Joseph's Day in March. The making of "altars" decorated with baked goods which are prepared in honor of St. Joseph and displayed, often in private homes, in elaborate tableaux with religious statuary and other sacred objects, is still a tradition in some families.

The terms "Italian" and "Roman Catholic" are practically synonymous to many Mississippi people because Italians make up a large part of the congregation in many of the Catholic churches in the state. In Bay St. Louis, which has a small Italian community, there is a special shrine to St. Mary on the grounds of the St. Rose de Lima church.

Indians

The number of families of Indian ancestry in Mississippi has grown in recent years. In the late 1960s, when Seetha Srinivasan and her husband Asoka arrived in Jackson, there were only eight or ten families. Today there are over two hundred. Many of the newcomers made their way here from former British colonies in Africa after spending a few years in England.[37] When the Srinivasans first came, most Indians in Mississippi were professionals, drawn here by hospitals and universities. Today the mix includes many owners of small businesses: motels, gas stations, dry cleaners, and ice cream parlors.

The centers of Indian ethnicity are the home and temple. Since the building of a temple in Brandon by the Hindu Temple Society of Mississippi, Inc., Indians have a place to maintain religious traditions, social ties, and children's Indian education. The practice of the Hindu religion is more relaxed than that of many other religions, and much of the observance and worship focuses on family relations. But having the temple and its full-time staff gives the Indian community a place to gather and pray. Membership in the Hindu association is over 350, but the number of Indians in the state is estimated to be several times that figure.

Traditional Indian customs of food and dress are important to most of these families. Many Indian women dress in the traditional manner, the sari being the most recognizable form of clothing to non–Indians. To supply the fabrics and ready–made clothing, as well as the special spices and foods for Indian cuisine, peddlers come from Nashville several times a year and set up shop in motel rooms.

Indians also keep up ties to family members living in India. Some travel there regularly and bring parents for visits to Mississippi. Indians follow political and social changes in their homeland, and some maintain professional ties. A scientist at the University Medical Center in Jackson, for example, might travel to India for a residency. And it is not uncommon for Indian doctors here to own stock in Indian hospitals.

Even with the interest in their land of origin, Indians are firmly rooted in Mississippi. According to D. Desaiah, many Indians emigrated to the United States "to improve their basic skills," and upon becoming professionals, showed their "willingness to settle down. Once they came, they put their heart into it."[38] When asked about his adjustment to living in the Delta, Mike Patel, manager of the Best Western Motel in Indianola, said, "We love it here. We would never think of leaving."[39]

Chinese

Around a hundred years ago, Chinese men were first brought to the Delta to become sharecroppers.[40] The work did not suit them, however, so many opened grocery stores, mostly in black neighborhoods. Being neither European/white nor African/black, the Chinese were caught in an ambiguous middle ground. Or as many Chinese prefer to see it, their own ground, which they sought, rather than be segregated by whites as colored.[41]

In the twentieth century, several Delta communities supported separate schools for Chinese children. The total enrollment of the two–room Chinese school in Cleveland in the mid–1940s was thirty–six students and three teachers, one of whom was Chinese. According to a curriculum statement, "Citizenship and health are stressed more than anything else. Most of the children live in the backs of stores."[42]

Wilson Wong, who grew up in the Delta in the 1950s, remembers his first encounter with this dichotomy. "As a kid, my first encounter with segregation signs was at a cafe in the Delta. It had one door for 'colored' and one door for 'white' and I didn't know which one to go into. I had to make a decision about whether I was white or colored. I didn't choose either. So I didn't go in. That exemplified . . . where the Chinese community was. This was a culture that was caught in between. We were accepted and rejected by both blacks and whites."[43] Since the 1950s, overt segregation has ended, but the Chinese community still occupies a position of being both within and apart from the society around them. Being both Chinese and American in Mississippi presents problems for the Chinese, but despite the pressures to "assimilate," they have managed to keep close ties to China and other Chinese communities in the United States.

Chinese cuisine is popular in many homes, made possible by industrious gardeners. Kam Chow, for example, has adapted Chinese techniques of intensive vegetable gardening to the Clarksdale land and climate. Almost all year, on a plot of land behind his grocery store measuring a few dozen square feet, he is able to grow enough bitter melon, beans, bok choy, broccoli, mustard, cucumber, and other vegetables to feed his family. During dry spells, his ingenious system of hoses carries condensed water from his air conditioner to the garden. Whenever Daniel Shing visits China he always brings back seeds for Kam Chow and other back–yard gardeners.[44]

Many families celebrate Chinese holidays throughout the year, especially the lunar new year and the August full moon. On special anniversaries and weddings they have large parties where the women dress in traditional clothing. Nine hundred people came to the wedding of Daniel Shing's nephew. Rarely, however, is there any outward show of these festivities, and there is little interaction with the broader community.[45]

The isolation may be changing. Four years ago, the city of Clarksdale offered Daniel Shing use of city facilities to stage a Chinese New Year's banquet. For the past three years, the banquet has been well attended. For Shing, personally, this event has meant greater involvement with the civic life of the community. He says that other Chinese are also becoming "more outgoing," and points to several Chinese businessmen in Clarksdale who have joined the Chamber of Commerce and other civic and cultural groups.[46]

Despite growing involvement with the non–Chinese society, some young Chinese continue to leave the community. According to Shing, "There is more opportunity elsewhere, especially now that so many receive professional degrees." But then he continues, "Years ago, they all wanted to move to California, but opportunities there are not as great as they used to be, so many are staying in the South."[47] Far from giving up Chinese culture, the young also show an interest in the language and culture. Shing himself is proof of this assertion: when family pressure to marry became too great, he went to Singapore to find a wife. The Shings maintain ties to their family in China, and they subscribe to several Chinese–language newspapers. Shing points with hope to the fact that Delta State University is now offering courses in Chinese for the first time.[48]

German

On his seventieth birthday in 1897, German immigrant Elisaeus von Seutter published a leaflet with a photograph of his garden in Jackson. In the photograph he poses with his wife amid century plant and palmetto, oleander and zinnia. The garden, states the inscription on the verso side, is his labor of love: "For thirty-two years have I labored here in the early mornings, and on Saturdays," he explains.[49] In the poem, which he wrote to accompany the photo, he describes his garden as a metaphor for his becoming rooted in his new home.

Von Seutter was one of dozens of Germans who settled in Mississippi in the nineteenth and twentieth centuries, many in the area of Gluckstadt, northwest of Jackson. The St. Joseph Catholic Church of Gluckstadt has about sixty families in its congregation, forty of whom claim German ancestry. Since the 1950s, the church has sponsored an annual festival to coincide with the Bavarian Oktoberfest. In recent years, the festival has become very popular, drawing 10,000 visitors in 1989 and 15,000 in 1990.[50] A similar festival is held yearly in Heidelberg, northeast of Laurel.

On the Gulf coast, the community of German families has grown rapidly in the past decade as families settle on the coast after retirement from military service. The German–American Society of the Gulf Coast sponsors an annual Oktoberfest as well, complete with a contest for the most authentic traditional *lederhosen* and *dirndl* costumes, and also a Folksmarch.[51]

Greeks

Arthur Fokakis arrived in Hattiesburg in 1920 with little money or knowledge of English, but he knew one thing—railroad men, businessmen, and workers in the Hub City needed to eat. He set up a fruit stand under a tree on Main Street, just across from the train station. Within a few years he was able to open a cafe, the Coney Island, which is still operated today by his grandson, Billy.[52]

The Fokakis story could serve as model for the experience of many Mississippians of Greek descent. "I couldn't speak English at the time [I came to the United States]," said James Zouboukos, owner of the Elite Restaurant in Jackson.[53] He first settled in Waco, Texas, in 1935 because three of his uncles already had a restaurant there. After serving in World War II, he and his brother Peter opened the Elite. Many Jackson restaurants are Greek.

The center of Greek life is the family and the church. "The Greek Orthodox Church was a place to worship, but it was also a place [of] fellowship with other Greeks," said Bill Vallas of Jackson, whose father, Theo, helped found the Greek Orthodox Holy Trinity St. John the Theologian Church there.[54] The Greek community on the Gulf Coast was also large enough to sustain a Greek Orthodox Church. The churches together sponsor an annual "Greek Night" in which the Greek community stages a feast with music and dancing and invites all to come, regardless of their heritage.

The Greeks on the Gulf Coast have never been a large community, but their influence has been great. For many years, during the Coast's heyday as "the Riviera of the South," many of the best restaurants were Greek–owned. With the destruction of many tourist attractions by Hurricane Camille in 1969, however, most of these establishments did not survive. Greeks have also been influential in professional and political life.[55]

Even with the passing of the first generation of Greek Mississippians, younger Greeks keep alive the customs, religious and otherwise. The recent wedding of a Greek man and a non–Greek woman was held in the man's church, the Greek Orthodox. Every New Year's Day the priest comes to bless every room of the couple's house. Thus the survival of Greek culture in Mississippi seems to be assured.

Looking Ahead

People living outside of Mississippi, as well as many Mississippians, are often surprised to learn that there is an "ethnic Mississippi." Ethnic communities in Mississippi do exist, and their presence in the state needs to be better understood. The experiences of those who identify themselves with a particular ethnic tradition while assimilating themselves into American cultures also need to be explored. Thus the project which led to this essay is not the culmination but is just the beginning of our work on "ethnic Mississippi."

Mississippi—A Multi-ethnic State

People living outside Mississippi and some Mississippians as well often perceive the state as a society of Anglo- and African- Americans. Although these two are the largest ethnic groups in Mississippi, they are joined by many others. Indeed the pattern of settlement of ethnic communities has remained consistent throughout the years. The most cohesive communities can be found in Mississippi River towns, in the Delta, along the Gulf Coast, and in the Jackson metropolitan area. The reasons for this distinct pattern are clear enough. New Orleans has always been a major port of entry for immigrants, so it is natural that they settled along the Mississippi River and the Gulf Coast. The Delta offered jobs to immigrants in the early years of this century when cotton farming was flourishing and towns developing. Jackson, the state capital and its largest city, offered job opportunities for immigrants. The Gulf Coast continues to attract immigrants who are looking for a coastal environment and economy, as in the case of the Slavonians, the Acadian French, the Greeks, the Italians, the Vietnamese, and most recently, Hispanics.

Even though the population of some groups has declined through outmigration and assimilation, the number of the groups themselves appears to be increasing. The Jewish population showed a steep decline in the past half–century necessitating the closing of temples in Natchez and other places, but Jewish communities in other areas, such as Clarksdale, now seem to be declining less quickly than before. The Lebanese community, on the other hand, has remained fairly stable over the years and shows little sign of losing members.

The same can be said for Greeks, Italians, Slavonians, and French Acadian. The Vietnamese, Indian, Choctaw, and Hispanic communities are actually growing. Thus the state's ethnic communities may change, but they are not likely to disappear.

As the society in Mississippi grows more diverse, so will its political and cultural life. As these groups seek involvement in the state's political system, they will undoubtedly present new ideas and needs. The complexities of Mississippi life will require of citizens a greater understanding and appreciation of its diverse population and its varied interests and needs. In the process, however, the texture of life for all will be enriched.

All photographs on the following pages are by D. C. Young unless otherwise noted.

Mississippi Choctaw men and women, c. 1908. Photograph by M. R. Harrington. Courtesy of the Museum of the American Indian, Heye Foundation.

Above: Arch Mingo, chanter for Choctaw dances, wearing traditional shirt, hat, and beadwork at the Mississippi Crafts Center on the Natchez Trace Parkway. 1987. *Right:* Albert Henry, Choctaw farmer, dressed for stickball, c. 1908. Photograph by M. R. Harrington. Courtesy of the Museum of the American Indian, Heye Foundation.

Left: Melvin Henry with baskets he makes from white oak cut from his land in Neshoba County. 1988. Henry learned basketmaking and other farming crafts from his father, Albert Henry. *Above:* Phillip Martin, chief of the Mississippi Choctaw, was elected to an unprecedented fourth term in 1991. His leadership, especially his advocacy of "Choctaw Self-determination," has helped the tribe find ways to be both American *and* Choctaw. 1988.

An example of Choctaw industry: Choctaw workers assembling the wiring for automobile dashboards, which requires the same skills as those used by traditional Choctaw craftsmen. This factory is located on the Choctaw reservation in Neshoba County. 1988.

Scottish bagpipe band at the annual Highland Festival sponsored by the Gulf Coast's Scottish, Irish, and English associations. 1990.

The Hibernia Society of the Gulf Coast, founded for primarily social reasons, has become an advocate of greater appreciation of Irish culture by the Coast's "Irish by consent." 1988.

Tommy Fairley leads the congregation of the Trinity House of
Prayer, Moorhead, in song. 1989.

"Juneteenth," the day news of the Emancipation Proclamation spread by word-of-
mouth across the South, is one of the
holidays celebrated by the African-
American community in Mississippi.
Hattiesburg businessman and civic leader,
Johnny DuPree, was King of Hattiesburg's Juneteenth in 1991. Accompanying
him is Lillie McLaurin, "Official Mother
of Hattiesburg," whose news stand on
Mobile Street has been a center of African life in the Hub City since 1946. 1991.

When he was a young man, B. B. King went
to town on Saturdays and played his guitar
and sang on this sidewalk in Indianola,
across from the Sunflower County court-
house. The spot's significance is com-
memorated with a painting by Indianola
artist and blues musician Bobby Whalen.
1991.

James "Son" Thomas of Leland carries two significant African artistic traditions—he is both a blues musician and a sculptor. His music in the practically extinct country style has won him worldwide acclaim; his sculptures, which are highly personal statements with links to older African traditions, are likewise held in high esteem by collectors. 1990.

Portia Labat and Sylvia Labat of Bay St. Louis are proud of their Creole French heritage. They maintain ties with Creole families in Louisiana and are active in the local historical society. 1991.

According to folklorists, the African aesthetic draws on the spirit of improvisation—and Earl Simmons's Art Shop in Bovina bears this out. Constructed of materials found and donated by friends, Earl's place is a mixture of old and new, junk and jewels. He also constructs assemblages out of found materials and sells them to passers-by. He is represented by galleries in Vicksburg and New Orleans. 1990.

Left: St. Rose de Lima Catholic Church, Bay St. Louis, was dedicated in 1926. It was named after the first saint from the western hemisphere to be canonized. The Holy Spirit Missionary Sisters established a school here for the town's African children. 1991. *Below:* Auseklis Ozols, *Transfiguration*, paint on plaster, 1991. St. Rose de Lima Catholic Church, Bay St. Louis. The "Black Christ of the Bay," as the painting is called by some, is actually a composite of all the ethnic groups in Bay St. Louis. The artist, himself an immigrant from Latvia, even had a Jewish friend pose for the naval. In the branches of the live oak, the names of the families of the parish have been inscribed.

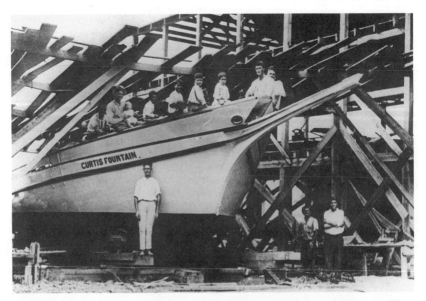

The Biloxi schooner *Curtis Fountain* under construction on Back Bay Biloxi, c. 1925. The Fountain family, one of the earliest French families to settle in Biloxi, has been important in the Coast's boatbuilding tradition. Photographer unknown. Courtesy of Biloxi Public Library.

Richard Desporte's family has operated a bakery in Biloxi for generations and has one of the South's oldest brick ovens. 1990.

The annual Mardi Gras parade staged in Biloxi by the Gulf Coast Carnival Association carries on the tradition of pre-Lenten revelry begun, so
it is said, by sailors of the d'Iberville expedition in 1699. 1990.

The Blessing of the Fleet brings together all the ethnic groups and traditions of Point
Cadet. The Shrimp King in 1991 was an Acadian. The contestants for Shrimp Queen in-
cluded Slavonian, Acadian, and Vietnamese girls. The pageant was held at the Fleur de
Lis Society Hall on Howard Avenue. 1991.

Above: A couple dances the Cajun Two-Step at the Seafood Festival, a celebration of the seafood industry's heritage sponsored by the Biloxi Seafood Industry Museum. The annual event focuses attention on the contributions of all the ethnic groups that have played a role in the development of the industry. 1989. *Left:* August DeRouen, Acadian net-maker, works on a cast net at the Biloxi Seafood Industry Museum. DeRouen was attracted to Biloxi in the 1920s by the opportunity for employment in the seafood industry. 1988.

Miguel Saavedra, a native of Mexico, helped
found the Hispanic Cultural Society on the Gulf
Coast. 1991.

A custom brought from Latin countries to Bay St. Louis is the whitewashing of family
tombs and gravestones on All Saints Day. 1988.

Above left: Anthony "Tony Jack" Covacevich, owner of the Covacevich Boat Yard on Back Bay Biloxi. His father, "Jacky Jack," immigrated to Biloxi with boat-building skills and learned to design and construct the local boat styles. The Covacevich yard constructed the most famous Biloxi schooner, the *Mary Margaret*, in 1928–1929. After winning the schooner race of 1930—hailed by all as the fastest ever seen—she sank in a storm off Ship Island. 1989. *Above:* Neil Covacevich, brother of Tony Jack, carries on the tradition of wooden boat-building at his yard on Point Cadet in Biloxi. He is currently constructing a schooner as part of the Biloxi Seafood Industry Museum's project to build two schooners like those which once comprised the Biloxi fishing fleet. 1989. *Below:* Slavonians in traditional costume. Biloxi, c. 1939. Photographer unknown. Courtesy of Mississippi Department of Archives and History.

Pusharata making at the Slavic Benevolent Association lodge, Point Cadet, Biloxi, 1988. The women's auxiliary of the association has, for many years now, prepared dozens of *pusharatas* and sold them to the public at Christmas. The occasion is social as well as profitable. Dozens of Slavonians and non-Slavonians drop by the lodge to pick up their Christmas Eve treats.

Vietnamese "chopstick" shrimp fishing boat. This method of shrimping, brought from Vietnam, was adapted for the shallow waters of Biloxi Bay and the Mississippi Sound. Vietnamese fishermen stage their own Blessing of the Fleet to coincide with Vietnamese holidays. 1988.

Terry Do, whose parents left Vietnam in 1975 as "boat people," enjoys Vietnamese cuisine, which his mother cooks almost exclusively. 1989.

Above: Shoppers in the Vietnamese market, Biloxi, 1988. *Right:* Ly Yen, owner of Tan Du Department Store, shows off one of the many suits for sale in his dry goods section, along with other clothing and silk fabrics. 1988. Tan Du, in Point Cadet, Biloxi, carries all the goods necessary for Vietnamese cooking and dress and for Buddhist religious observance.

Minh Duc, a leader of the Vietnamese community, explains the various foods prepared especially for Tet and served to all who come to the Buddhist temple. 1991.

This Buddhist temple in Biloxi, was formerly a private residence in the Point Cadet neighborhood. 1991.

The dragon visits Tan Du Department Store during Tet. 1991.

Above: Vietnamese gravesite, Biloxi Cemetery. 1988. *Bottom right:* Vietnamese workers take a break. Photograph 1990 by Michelle Stonecypher.

Left: Jewish cemetery, Vicksburg. 1991. *Above:* Aaron Kline, Clarksdale, has been a leader of the Jewish community since his arrival in 1935 from Latvia. 1991.

The gravestone of Raphael Dreyfuss (d. 1862) stands next to markers commemorating the Siege of Vicksburg. 1991.

Joe Martin Erber (l.), a long-time employee of the Post Office, and Meyer Gelman, a retired local clothier, are keepers of the last Orthodox *shul,* Congregation Ahavath Rayim, in Greenwood. Photograph by Bill Aron. Courtesy of Museum of the Southern Jewish Experience, Utica, MS. 1989.

Thomas "Fab" Farris and a photograph of his family around 1920. His father had come to the U.S. years before, when he was eighteen. "Fab" is the boy in center wearing a cap. 1991.

Bubba Mohamed, Inverness, operates Mohamed's dry goods store. His father left Lebanon to escape conscription into the Sultan's army. His brother, Ollie, is a member of the Mississippi state senate. 1991.

Louise Chamoun, Clarksdale, preparing Lebanese dishes, *kibbie* and stuffed grape leaves, in the kitchen of the restaurant she and her husband Chafik own. 1991.

J. M. Nosser and Sons grocery store has been in this building since 1924. In addition to the usual merchandise, the store stocks Lebanese staples such as cracked wheat and bulgar. 1991.

The first Cruso seafood packing plant, c. 1925. Point Cadet, Biloxi. Photographer unknown. Courtesy of Lillie Lancon.

Lee and Guiseppe Cuicchi driving "the first tractor in Shaw," c. 1925. Malatesta family collection. Courtesy of Mississippi Department of Archives and History.

Above: Lillie Lancon, an Italian who married an Acadian, stirs gumbo in the kitchen of the family restaurant on Point Cadet. 1989. *Right:* Gino Scialdone, president of the Italian American Association of Gulfport, preparing spaghetti for the annual Italian American Cultural Festival. 1990.

Fratesi Grocery, Highway 82, Leland. Many Italians settled and remain in the Shaw-Leland area of the Delta. In Greenville the Italian Association sponsors Sunday *bocce* games. 1991.

Bocce, the Italian lawn-bowling game, is played wherever there is an Italian community. This game was part of a tournament at the Italian Cultural Heritage Festival in Gulfport. 1990.

At the Hindu Temple, Brandon, women chant during services honoring the birth of the god Ganesha. 1991.

The priest of the Hindu Temple in Brandon distributes coconut milk during services honoring the birth of the god Ganesha. 1991.

Kam Chow, Clarksdale, plants his intensive garden according to Chinese techniques. In the summer, he diverts condensation runoff (from his grocery store's air conditioner) to his garden. Kam Chow's large melons hang from an overhead scaffolding, their weight supported by bricks and boards. The melons are numbered so that they may be harvested in the proper order. 1991.

Johnny Choo's family has been in the grocery business in the Delta since the 1920s. Choo, a graduate of Mississippi State University, is the owner of Greenville's largest and most popular supermarket, Bing's Supervalu. He is active in civic affairs; among the Chinese holiday cards and good luck fish displayed in his store are citations for public service. Although Choo's grocery employs 110 people, it is still a family business. Choo's father-in-law and mother-in-law both work there, stocking shelves and checking out customers. In contrast to Americans, the Chinese do not separate work from personal life. 1989.

Elisaeus von Seutter and his wife, Jackson, 1897. Photograph by Elisaeus von Seutter. Courtesy of Mississippi Department of Archives and History.

The Fokakis family at the Coney Island Cafe, Hattiesburg. Arthur's grandson, Billy, operates the cafe today. 1991.

James Vasselus arrived in Hattiesburg from Greece in 1912 and opened a fruit stand where the railroads crossed. His younger brother Paul came in 1915, and together they opened the California Sandwich Shop, which is still operated by their descendants. Paul Vasselus is the man on the right wearing a bow tie, c. 1940. Photographer unknown. Courtesy of California Sandwich Shop.

Notes

1. The series of photographs taken by M.R. Harrington in 1907 as part of an ethnographic study for the Smithsonian Institution provide a remarkable view into the lives of Choctaws at the turn of the century. They have not been published but are available through the Museum of the American Indian, Heye Foundation.

2. David Hackett Fischer, *Albion's Seed: Four British Folkways in America* (Oxford: Oxford University Press, 1989).

3. Grady McWhiney, "Antebellum Piney Woods Culture: Continuity Over Time and Place," in *Mississippi's Piney Woods: A Human Perspective*, ed. Noel Polk (Jackson: University Press of Mississippi, 1986), 41.

4. St. Peter's Church, Bassfield, Mississippi, "A History of St. Peter's, Bassfield" (1975), 2–3.

5. Laddie Weems, Personal Interview, 14 November 1988, and Edmund Boudreau, Personal Interview, 16 November 1990.

6. Boudreau interview.

7. Miguel Saavedra, Personal Interview, 28 September 1991.

8. *Ibid.*

9. *Ibid.*

10. *Ibid.*

11. Tom Rankin, Personal Interview, 23 August 1991.

12. Anthony V. Ragusin, Personal Interview, 16 November 1990.

13. Tony Jack Covacevich, Personal Interview, 16 November 1990.

14. Jackie Gilich, Personal Interview, 15 November 1990.

15. Neville Broussard, Personal Interview, 20 May 1989.

16. Minh Duc, Personal Interview, 14 February 1991.

17. Museum of the Southern Jewish Experience, "Images of Southern Jewish Life, Tour I: Louisiana and Mississippi." Exhibit text; photographs by Bill Aron.

18. Aron Kline, Personal Interview, 24 August 1991.

19. Charlotte Graham, "Determined to Succeed," *Clarion-Ledger* (Jackson, Mississippi), 26 January 1991, sec. D.

20. Katie Abbott and Biffie Brewer, "Brett Silverblatt Has Bat-mitzvah," *Enterprise-Tocsin* (Indianola, Mississippi), 14 September 1989, sec. 2.

21. Goldie Hirshberg, Personal Interview, 24 August 1991.

22. James Watts, "Blast Probe in 4th Day, March Held," *Clarion-Ledger* (Jackson, Mississippi), 22 September 1967; Mrs. Robert D. Levy, "Temple Blast Could Be a Bell That Tolls for All of Jackson," *Clarion-Ledger* (Jackson, Mississippi), 23 September 1967.

23. Museum of the Southern Jewish Experience, "Keeping the Story Alive," n.d.

24. Queenie Nossour, quoted in Deborah Skipper, "Lebanese-American Families Knit Future from Past," *Clarion-Ledger* (Jackson, Mississippi), 18 September 1983, sec. E.

25. Chafik Chamoun, Personal Interview, 23 August 1991.
26. Nossour, quoted in Skipper "Lebanese-American."
27. Nicholas Saikley, Personal Interview, 18 August 1991.
28. *Ibid.*
29. *Ibid.*
30. Thomas Farris, Personal Interview, 23 August 1991.
31. *Ibid.*
32. Nicholas Saikley, Personal Interview, 18 August 1991.
33. Chuck Abraham, quoted in Skipper "Lebanese-American."
34. Lillie Cruso Lancon, Personal Interview, 15 November 1990.
35. Gino Scialdone, Personal Interview, 29 November 1990.
36. Jeff Edwards, "That's Amore." *Clarion-Ledger* (Jackson, Mississippi), 24 January 1991, sec. D.
37. Seetha Srinivasan, Personal Interview, 9 August 1991.
38. D. Desaiah, quoted in Deborah Skipper, "Indians Put Their Heart in Homeland, *Clarion-Ledger* (Jackson, Mississippi), 21 September 1983, sec. C.
39. Mike Patel, quoted in Skipper "Indians."
40. Sid Graves, Personal Interview, 23 August 1991; Daniel Shing, Personal Interview, 23 August 1991.
41. Robert Seto Quan, *Lotus Among the Magnolias* (1982).
42. "Schools at War: Report to the Nation." Unpublished scrapbook. Mississippi Department of Archives and History.
43. Wilson Wong, quoted in Leslie Myers, "The Delta Draw," *Clarion-Ledger* (Jackson, Mississippi) 22 January 1991, sec. C.
44. Shing interview.
45. *Ibid.*
46. *Ibid.*
47. *Ibid.*
48. *Ibid.*
49. Elisaeus von Seutter, "Ein Stucken Heim und Familie," (1897).
50. Evelyn Smith, "Yearly Festival Proves Almost Too Popular," *Clarion-Ledger* (Jackson, Mississippi), 25 September 1989, sec. A; Sherry Lucas, "Gluckstadt's Germ of Idea Grew Into Bratwurst Brouhaha," *Clarion-Ledger* (Jackson, Mississippi), 19 September 1991, sec. E.
51. "Eins. . . Zwei. . . G'Suffa," *Biloxi-D'Iberville Press*, 25 September 1991; "Mayor Pete Halat," *Biloxi-D'Iberville Press*, 25 September 1991.
52. Arthur Fokakis, Personal Interview, 7 April 1990.
53. James Zouboukos, Personal Interview, 12 June 1990.
54. Bill Vallas, Personal Interview, 12 June 1990.
55. Mrs. Kosta Vlahos, Personal Interview, 12 June 1990.

Contributors

Barbara Carpenter is Assistant Director of the Mississippi Humanities Council. In this capacity she administers a state-wide grant program and directs and edits all council publications. She holds the Ph.D. in modern literature from Tulane University and a master's degree in American literature from the University of Georgia, where she studied as a Woodrow Wilson Scholar. She taught college English at schools in Louisiana and Mississippi before coming to the council. Carpenter has been involved in planning programming for the Columbus Quincentenary for the last five years and has served on state, regional, and national committees and programs on this topic.

William Cash, chair of the Department of History at Delta State University, holds the Ph.D. from the University of Alabama. Cash is a frequent contributor and reviewer for scholarly publications, serving on the editorial board of *The Journal of Mississippi History,* and active in numerous professional organizations. His most recent publications include the *History of the Delta Council* and *My Dear Nellie,* a collection of letters he edited jointly with Judge Lucy Howorth.

Patricia Galloway is Special Projects Officer at the Mississippi Department of Archives and History who received her Ph.D. from the University of North Carolina at Chapel Hill. A prolific scholar in early Choctaw history, Galloway has won numerous awards for her research and writing. She edited the *Mississippi Provincial Archives: French Dominion Project* and is currently editor of several scholarly journals, including the proceedings of the French colonial Historical Society. Her recent publications include "The Archaeology of Historical Narrative" in *Columbian Consequences, III,* "The Chief Who Is Your Father" in *Powhatan's Mantle,* and *Southeastern Ceremonial Complex,* which she edited for the University of Nebraska Press. Nebraska will also publish her forthcoming *Choctaw Genesis, 1500–1700.* Galloway is a popular lecturer and presenter at professional conferences and moving force in the Mississippi Columbus Quincentenary Committee.

Paul E. Hoffman, professor of history at Louisiana State University, holds the Ph.D. from the University of Florida. His extensive publications include *The Spanish Crown and the Defense of the Caribbean, 1535–1585, A New Andalucia and a Way to the Orient,* and "The Historian and Historic Sites in Archaeology," in *Forgotten Places and Things: Archaeological Perspectives on American History.* He has recently contributed several articles to the Columbus Encyclopedia. An active member of the profession, Hoffman served on the faculty of the NEH Summer Institute on Southeastern Indians held at the University of Georgia in 1989 and 1990.

Robert Jenkins, Associate Professor of History at Mississippi State University, specializes in African-American and Mississippi history. His recent publications include "African Americans on the Natchez Trace, 1800–1865" in *The Southern Quarterly* and "The Black Land Grant in the Formative Years, 1890–1920" in *Agricultural History.* An article entitled "The Nazis in the American South: A Mirror Image?" is forthcoming in *The Journal of Southern History.* Jenkins has participated in Mississippi Humanities Council activities for many years and is a popular lecturer.

Jay K. Johnson, Professor of Anthropology and Associate Director of the Center for Archaeological Research at the University of Mississippi, received the Ph.D. from Southern Illinois University. Johnson has been involved in numerous excavations in the Southeast and subsequent site reports and has published extensively in scholarly journals. His major publications include *The Organization of Core Technology* and the forthcoming *Development of Southeastern Archaeology.* He is currently working on material excavated from prehistoric and historic Chickasaw sites and has an ongoing interest in the archaic period. Johnson received NEH funding for satellite studies of the area in 1990.

Clara Sue Kidwell is Associate Professor of American studies at the University of California at Berkeley, on leave for 1992 at the University of California Humanities Research Institute at Irvine. She was awarded the Ph.D. from the University of Oklahoma. In 1989, Kidwell and Galloway received NEH funding to research Indian land holdings in Mississippi. Her publications include "Science and Ethnoscience" (*Indian History*), "Indian Education" in *American Education: A Sociological View,* and "American Indian Attitudes Toward Nature" (*Contemporary Native American Attitudes*). She is currently completing a manuscript on *Choctaws and Missionaries in Mississippi* for the University of Tennessee Press and continues work on the Choctaw land claims after 1830.

Charles D. Lowery, Professor and Department Head, Department of History, Mississippi State University, holds the Ph.D. from the University of Virginia. A specialist in the colonial and territorial period, Lowery has published widely in early Mississippi history. His publications include *James Barbour: The Biography of a Jeffersonian Republican,*"The Great Migration to the Mississippi Territory, 1798–1819" (*Journal of Mississippi History*), and "Religion in America: The Contemporary Scene." The *Encyclopedia of African-American Civil Rights, from Emancipation to the Present,* edited with John Marszalak, is forthcoming from Greenwood Press in 1992; works in progress include *Jamie Whitten: The Voice of Agriculture in the House,* with Roy V. Scott. He is a former member of the MHC.

John H. Peterson, Jr., is Professor of Anthropology at Mississippi State University. He completed his doctoral dissertation for the University of Georgia in 1970 based on a year of field research with the Mississippi Choctaws. Since then he has published extensively on Choctaw history as well as working for the tribal government full-time for one year and serving as advisor for many years. His interest in the development of Indian self-government was recently extended by a Fulbright Senior Lectureship to the University of Zimbabwe where he undertook field research on the development of local governmental institutions in a newly-independent African nation. Peterson's publications include *A Choctaw Source Book,* "Indians in the South," in *Red White, and Black: Indians in the Old South;*"Evolution and Consequences of a Technological Change Program in Rural Mississippi (*Anthropological Approaches to Change*), and "Mississippi Choctaw Identity: Genesis and Change" in *The New Ethnicity.* He is a member of the MHC.

Robert S. Weddle is a specialist in Spanish and French colonial history of the Gulf Coast. His recent books, *La Salle, the Mississippi, and the Gulf: Three Primary Documents* and *Spanish Sea: The Gulf of Mexico in North American Discovery*, published by Texas A & M University Press, were supported by NEH grants. A prolific independent scholar, Weddle has also published *The San Saba Mission: Spanish Pivot in Texas, San Juan Bautista: Gateway to Spanish Texas*, and *Wilderness Manhunt: The Spanish Search for La Salle*.

Samuel J. Wells, III, holds the Ph.D. in history from the University of Southern Mississippi, where his dissertation topic was Choctaw treaties during the American territorial period. He currently teaches at Pearl River Community College and pursues historical research with his wife, Mary Ann Wells. He was joint editor with Roseanna Tubby of *After Removal: The Choctaw in Mississippi* and contributed the chapter on "The Role of Mixed Bloods in Choctaw History." Other publications include "Treaties and the Choctaw People" (*Choctaw Tribal Government: A New Era*), "Counting Countrymen on the Tombigbee" (*The Southern Historian*), which won the Kenneth R. Wesson Award, and "Rum, Skins, and Powder," which appeared in *The Chronicles of Oklahoma*.

D. C. Young is a free-lance photographer in Hattiesburg, Mississippi. She and her husband, Stephen Young, have produced several exhibits and exhibit catalogues for Mississippi Humanities Council programs in recent years, notably *Biloxi's Ethnic Heritage: Images of Changes and Tradition* and "Biloxi Vietnamese." Her photographs have appeared in such publications as *New Arts Review, Mississippi Choctaw Crafts, Woman's World*, and *Mississippi Crafts*. She is a very popular member of the MHC Speakers Bureau. The Youngs have recently made joint presentations on their work at the Southeast College Art Association and International Visual Sociologists Association conferences.

Stephen Young, a cultural historian, is editor of *The Southern Quarterly* and regional editor of *Arts Papers*. His wide range of interests has led him to serve as program administrator at the Mississippi Arts Commission, writer-in-residence at the Craftsman's Guild of Mississippi, director and curator at various arts centers and museums, and historian and history teacher at institutions throughout the South. He and D. C. Young have been involved in a number of MHC-funded projects on Mississippi ethnic culture, including

"Biloxi Vietnamese" and "Biloxi's Ethnic Heritage," "Delta Blues Today," "Sunflower Gospel Today," and "Mississippi Yard Show: Vernacular Perspectives." He publishes extensively in arts publications, scholarly journals, and popular magazines, and belongs to numerous professional organizations.

Index